County Sligo in 1837

A Topographical Dictionary

Extracts from

"A Topographical Dictionary of Ireland"

By

Samuel Lewis

Published by
The County Sligo Heritage and
Genealogy Society

2003

County Sligo in 1837

Tel: (071) 9143728
Email: heritagesligo@eircom.net

ISBN: 0-9545506-0-9

Printed by: Carrick Print, Carrick-on-Shannon

COVER ILLUSTRATIONS

Front:
Ballinafad Castle / Banada Abbey (Wakeman Prints)

Back:
Map of County Sligo showing Baronies in colour. (Grierson, 1816)

(Courtesy of Sligo Co. Library)

Foreword

BY REV. FRANCIS M. BEIRNE

Chairperson of the County Sligo Heritage & Genealogy Society

The history of the nineteenth century of Ireland has been well documented in statistical data, prose, verse, fiction, lyrics, monument and folklore. We have been fortunate to have the perception and scholarship of some outstanding authors whose imagination, ingenuity and appreciation of our environmental heritage inspired them to record detailed accounts of the people, events and places that were instrumental in the formation of Irish history during the nineteenth century.

The nineteenth century in particular was a tumultuous period here in Ireland with events that were set to become a defining point in the history of our island. It was a time of thriving enterprise but equally a time of horrendous depression and poverty. It was during this era that people struggled to establish their basic human rights and vigorously campaigned for equal opportunities for all Irish citizens. The nineteenth century will be remembered as a time of liberalisation from oppressive laws and the beginning of sowing seeds of a New Ireland, which is now coming to fruition. Whilst the nineteenth century was clouded with some regrettable events, nevertheless, it will always be a period that will intrigue and fascinate the minds and imagination of countless Irish people at home and throughout the world.

We are all products of our time with each successive generation deriving its origins and character from those gone before us. We are part of a great human chain of history each one providing that vital link with the past but simultaneously forging links with those who will come after us. However, we must constantly glance back for understanding and courageously stride forward hoping for opportunity and achievement.

The core of our history is undoubtedly rooted in our local parish history, which is statistically and graphically recorded, in the local parish registers, school roll books, memorial inscriptions, folklore and storied accounts handed down through generations. The greater volumes of published histories glaze over local happenings and invariably deprive us of the single greatest source of historical information. It is for that reason that Samuel Lewis' *"Topographical Dictionary of Ireland"*, originally published in 1837, is singularly one of the most treasured and sought after sources of Irish history. It uniquely combines both the national and local history of Ireland in two volumes and provides us with one of the most comprehensive and resourceful accounts of local history. Samuel Lewis, together with his numerous local history contributors, has rendered an outstanding service to Ireland in compiling this topographical account of every county, providing and extensive compendium of historical detail of every Irish town and parish as well as the less well known places of Ireland. Whilst Lewis and his contributors relied on earlier surveys, statistical and otherwise, nothing as encyclopaedic has been published since then. It has been a treasure trove for countless historians and researchers over the centuries.

We are now deeply indebted to the County Sligo Heritage and Genealogy Society who had the foresight to extract all Sligo related historical data from the two volumes of the Dictionary and compiled for us this well illustrated Sligo edition of Lewis' *"Topographical Dictionary"*. This practical and imaginative initiative will be greeted with much enthusiasm and great expectation. The information contained in the two volumes will now be far more accessible to a wider population of people and one will no longer be required to go to the reference library to avail of the original source. It will mean that the data related to Sligo in the Topographical Dictionary will have a far wider readership among historians, researchers, students and all who have an interest in the history of Sligo at heart. It will no doubt have huge implications for the promotion of a greater awareness and interest in local history and hopefully will prompt more communities to undertake the compilation of their own parish history. This laudable project was the brainchild of the County Sligo Heritage and Genealogy Society and generously funded by the Heritage Council as well as FAS the Employment and Training Authority of Sligo. However, let us not forget the initial work of research spearheaded by the late Samuel Lewis (obit. 1865) and his history contributors from practically every village across the length and breadth of Ireland who made the publication of this current edition such an easy task. We salute their enormous contribution to the preservation of our heritage and hope that this latest commendable publication will further perpetuate their memory and be an acknowledgement of our grateful appreciation of their invaluable work in recording a memorable period of history of Ireland.

Francis M. Beirne
13th August 2003

AKNOWLEDGEMENTS

County Sligo Heritage & Genealogy Society gratefully acknowledge the support of the Heritage Council, FAS, Sligo Leader Partnership Board, Sligo County Council, Mr Donal Tinney, Sligo County Librarian, Ms Siobhan Ryan, Heritage Officer, Mr. John O'Hara, members of our Committee and Staff and all others who assisted in the production of this volume.

SUPPORTED BY THE HERITAGE COUNCIL

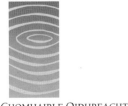

LE CUIDIÚ AN CHOMHAIRLE OIDHREACHTA

NATIONAL DEVELOPMENT PLAN

Introduction

by John C. McTernan

"A Topographical Dictionary of Ireland" by Samuel Lewis was published in London in 1837 as one of a series covering England, Scotland and Wales. It is doubtless the most comprehensive description of the country in pre Famine times and contains statistics from the 1831 census as well as detailed information on antiquities and history, agriculture and industry, public buildings, churches and schools in addition to the seats of the nobility.

The aim of the text was to give in a condensed form, "a faithful and impartial description of each place," which was contributed by a team of local contributors, many of whom were also subscribers. Mc Parlan's "Statistical Survey of County Sligo" (1801) was among the publications consulted in the compilation of the "Dictionary".

This edition of the extracts pertaining to County Sligo from Lewis' 1400 page two volume *"Topographical Dictionary"* contains descriptions of the Towns, Villages, and Parishes of the County and are reprinted here in the original format. Occasional mistakes in the text have been identified and corrected and the spelling of some place names, often scarcely identifiable, have been amended to coincide with modern usage. The only addition to the text is the inclusion of a number of prints and drawings which are interspersed here and there to embellish and compliment the text.

The names of the original subscribers – one hundred and twenty six of whom relate to County Sligo – have been extracted and reprinted on the basis that the list not only contains probable contributors but also a cross section of Sligonians of another era who pledged themselves to assist in the publication of a momentuous undertaking and a unique compilation.

Samuel Lewis carried on the business of a publisher under the style of Samuel Lewis & Co, at Aldergate Street, and later at Finsbury Park South, in London, over a number of years. His most widely known publications included *"A Topographical Dictionary of England"* (1831) *"A Topographical Dictionary of Wales"* (1833) *"A Topographical Dictionary of Ireland"* (1837) *"Atlas of Ireland"* (1837) and *"Atlas of England and Wales"* (1842). Lewis died in February 1865, and publication of topographical works was continued by his son, Samuel, the younger.

Illustrations

COUNTY SLIGO SUBSCRIBERS, 1837

Allen, William, Recorder of Sligo, Sligo.

Anderson, Richard, Sligo.

Armstrong, John, Justice of the Peace, Chaffpool, Ballymote.

Baker, Andrew, Redhill, Gurteen.

Beatty, David, Sligo & Dublin.

Beatty, James, Prison Governor, Sligo.

Bennett, William, Sligo.

Black, Joseph, Sligo.

Bolton, Henry, Ballyweelin, Rosses Point.

Boyle, James, Sligo.

Brennan, Malachi, Parish Priest, Carney.

Brennan, Peter, Parish Priest, Killaraght, Boyle.

Brereton, Robert P., Castletown, Easkey.

Brett, John, Tubbercurry.

Burke, Patrick D.D., Bishop of Elphin.

Caldwell, James, Sligo.

Campbell, James, Wine St., Sligo.

Chambers, William C., Cloverhill.

Clifford, H.I., Lieutenant, Thornhill, Sligo.

Cogan, Bernard O., Lisconny House, Riverstown.

Cogan, Edward H., Rockbrook, Riverstown.

Connolly, Felix, Reverend, Riverstown.

Cooper, Arthur B., Coopershill.

Corley, John, Catholic Curate, Kilshalvey.

Coulter, Samuel, Medical Doctor, Carney.

Crofton, James Sir, Longford House.

Crompton, John, Lieutenant, Dromore West.

Culbertson, David, Sligo.

Cullinan, Luke, Reverend, Kilross.

Dawson, John, Reverend, Easkey Vicarage.

Dodwell, George, Kevinsfort.

Donlevy, James, Parish Priest, Sligo.

Dowdican, Peter, Parish Priest, Dromard.

COUNTY SLIGO SUBSCRIBERS, 1837

Dubourdieu, Capt. Francis., Sligo.
Duke, John, Clogher, Boyle.
Durkan, Patrick, Parish Priest, Collooney.
Ellis, Thomas, Sligo.
Fahey, James, Reverend, Killoran.
Faussett, William, Willsboro, Sligo.
Feeney, Owen, Catholic Curate, Sligo.
Fenton, George, Dromore West.
Fenton, John, Dromore West.
Fenton, Thomas, Castletown, Easkey.
Ferrall, James J.C., Gibraltar House, Sligo.
Flannelly, Patrick, Parish Priest, Easkey.
Gallagher, J., Parish Priest, Mullinabreena, Achonry.
Garrett, Henry, Ballymote.
Garrett, John, Vicar, Emlaghfad.
Gore-Booth, Robert Sir, Lissadell.
Griffith, Henry, Ballytivnan House, Sligo.
Grove, William, Reverend, Charlesfort, Dromore West.
Hamilton, William, Sligo.
Harvey, George, Sligo.
Healy, Thomas, Parish Priest, Kilshalvey.
Henry, J & D., Sligo.
Hillas, William Hutchinson, Seaview House, Dromore West.
Holmes, Richard, Clogher, Monasteraden.
Homan, Travers, Colga, Sligo.
Hopkins, Rev Andrew, P.P,Castleconnor.
Horn, William, Sligo.
Hutchinson, Wm, Seaview House, Dromore, Co.Sligo.
Irwin, Henry, Medical Doctor, Sligo.
Irwin, Jones, Muckelty, Achonry.
Jones, Booth, Streedagh.
Jones, Jeremy, Seamount, Sligo.
Jones, John, Rockley Lodge, Sligo.
Jones, Robert, Fortland, Easkey.

COUNTY SLIGO SUBSCRIBERS, 1837

Jones, Vaughan, Donaughatraine, Dromore West.
Kelly, Andrew, Camphill, Collooney.
Kelly, Edward, Sligo.
Kenny, Terence, Catholic Curate, Ballyrush.
King, Robert, Cregg, Rosses Point.
Knott, Edward, Medical Doctor, Sligo.
Knott, Edward, Attyville, Ballymote.
Leader, H., Dromore West.
Mc Donnell, P., Cannaghanally, Dromore West.
Mc Hale, Patrick, Catholic Curate, Skreen.
Mc Hugh, John, Parish Priest, Ahamlish.
Mc Lester, Edward, Sligo.
Madden, Martin, Sligo.
Magauran, Peter, Reverend, Killery, Dromahair.
Manly, Michael, Sligo.
Martin, John, Member of Parliament, Sligo.
Martin, John Charles, Ellenville, Sligo.
Meredith, George, Primrose Grange, Sligo
Meredith, Joseph, Cloonamahon, Collooney
Mullarkey, Daniel, Parish Priest, Kilmacteigue.
Neynoe, William B., Colonel, Castleneynoe, Collooney.
Noone, Dominick, Catholic Curate, Ahamlish.
O'Callaghan, Michael, Parish Priest, Drumcliffe.
O'Connor, Charles, Church Hill, Sligo.
O'Connor, James, Reverend, Tubbercurry.
O'Connor, Peter, Sligo.
O'Donnell, James, Sligo.
O'Hara, Charles Kean, Annaghmore, Collooney.
O'Keane, Bernard, Parish Priest, Ballymote.
Ormsby, John, Castledargan, Collooney.
Ormsby, Thomas, Cummin, Sligo.
Ormsby, W., Farrellmacfarrell, Dromore West.
Orr, Robert, Lisdogan, Ballymote.
Paget, James, Kinniard, Enniscrone.

COUNTY SLIGO SUBSCRIBERS, 1837

Patterson, Edward, Shannon, Sligo.
Phibbs, William, Seafield, Sligo.
Rea, John, Grayfort, Ballymote.
Robinson, Samuel, Cloonbarry, Aclare.
Shaw, George, Kilsellagh, Sligo.
Sherlock, W.T., Mount Irwin, Gurteen.
Sim, Alexander, Collooney.
Simmonds, Joseph C., Sligo.
Simpson, James C., Millbrook, Sligo.
Soden, James, Moneygold, Grange.
Stack, John, Reverend, Dromard Glebe, Ballisodare.
Tempany, Myles, Sligo.
Thornley, Thomas, Lieutenant, Sligo.
Tracy, W.S., Sligo.
Trulock, George, Rectory, Skreen.
Tyler, Robert George, Sligo.
Vernon, Henry, Marino Cottage, Sligo.
Walsh, Matthew, Glen Lodge, Sligo.
West, Charles, Reverend, Grange.
White, James, Parish Priest, Kilmacshalgan, Dromore West
Wood, James, Woodville, Sligo.
Wood, William C., Finisklin.
Wynne, Owen, Hazelwood, Sligo.
Wynne, Richard Beavor, Sligo.

A
TOPOGRAPHICAL DICTIONARY

Of

IRELAND

COMPRISING THE

SEVERAL COUNTIES, CITIES, BOROUGHS, CORPORATE, MARKET, AND
POST TOWNS, PARISHES, AND VILLAGES,

WITH

HISTORICAL AND STATISTICAL DESCRIPTIONS;

Embellished With
ENGRAVINGS OF THE ARMS OF THE CITIES, BISHOPRICKS, CORPORATE
TOWNS, AND BOROUGHS; AND THE SEALS OF THE
SEVERAL MUNICIPAL CORPORATIONS:

With An
APPENDIX
DESCRIBING THE ELECTORAL BOUNDARIES OF THE SEVERAL
BOROUGHS, AS DEFINED BY THE ACT OF THE 2D & 3D OF WILLIAM IV.

BY SAMUEL LEWIS

IN TWO VOLUMES

LONDON:
Published By S. Lewis & Co. 87, Aldersgate Street.

MDCCCXXXVII

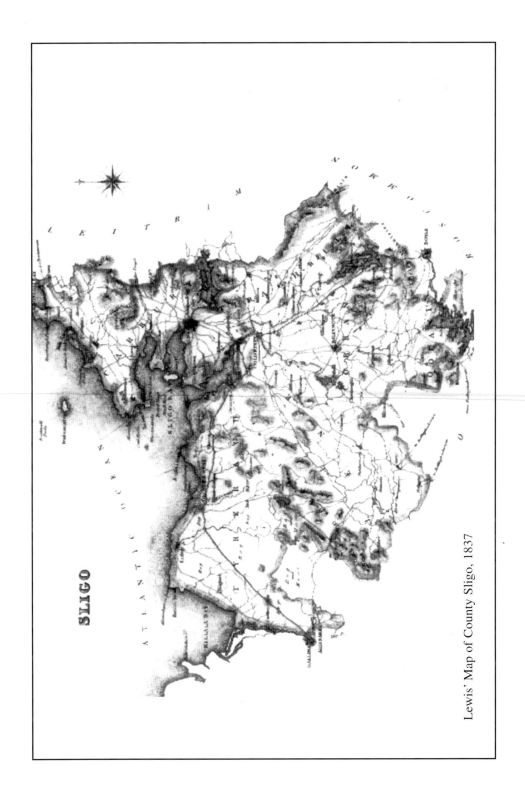

Lewis' Map of County Sligo, 1837

COUNTY OF SLIGO

Sligo is a maritime county of the province of Connaught bounded on the east by Leitrim, on the North by the Atlantic Ocean, on the South East by Roscommon. It extends from 530 53' 540 26' (N. Lat.) and from 80 3' to 90 1'(W. Lon.); and comprises an area, according to the Ordnance survey , of 434,188 statute acres, of which 257,217 are cultivated land, 168,711 are unimproved mountain and bog, and 8,260 are under water. The population in 1821 amounted to 146,229; and in 1831, to 171,508.

This County was included in the territory of the *Nagnatae* in the time of Ptolemy, the chief city of which tribe *Nagnatae* is supposed by some to have been somewhere near the site of the town of Sligo. It was afterwards possessed by a branch of the O' Conors , called for the sake of distinction O'Conor Sligo. The families of O'Hara, O'Dowd, Mac Donagh, and Mac Firbis, were also heads of septs in different districts. After the landing of the English under Henry 11., it gradually fell together with the rest of Connaught, into the hands of the great English leaders, of whom the Burghs or De Burgos were the most powerful in these parts. Yet this revolution was not effected without a protracted struggle, in the course of which a great battle was fought at Assadar, now Ballysadare, where O'Neill dynast of Tyrone was defeated, with great slaughter in an attempt to restore Cathal Caobhdearg to the throne of Connaught, from which he had been driven by Charles Carragh, aided by William De Burgo. Not many years after the site of the present town of Sligo being deemed a suitable position for defence, a castle was erected there in 1245, by Maurice-Fitzgerald, then Lord Deputy, which was destroyed in 1271, by O'Donnell, but rebuilt in the beginning of the ensuing century by Richard, Earl of Ulster. The county was regarded as part of Connaught, which, with, the exception of Roscommon, was then also considered by the English as a single county, until the 11th of Elizabeth, when the province was divided into seven counties of which Sligo was made one. About the same time O Conor Sligo had tendered his submission to Sir Henry Sidney, Lord deputy, and had obtained a grant of his lands under the crown of England at a rent of £100 per annum with a covenant to pay five horses and 130 bevees every Michaelmas in lieu of cess, and to bring twenty horsemen and forty foot soldiers into the field whenever summoned to attend a general hosting. During the disturbances by which the north and west of Ireland was distracted at the close of Elizabeth's reign, several actions took place in the county, in one of which the monastery of Ballymote was burned by the Irish. But the most remarkable incident connected with the County at that period was the defeat and death of Sir Conyers Clifford, who had succeeded Sir Richard Bingham in the presidency of Connaught; he had been sent by the Earl of Essex to Belleek. At the head of 1400 foot and a body of horse, consisting of 100 English and a number of Irish auxiliaries: In proceeding through the Curlew mountains, he pushed forward with his infantry through a defile, where he was suddenly attacked by O' Rourke, chieftain of Breffini, at the head of about 200 men, with such impetuosity that he was killed on the spot, together with several of his officers and 120 men, and the rest were driven back upon the cavalry, whose appearance checked the pursuit, and gave the fugitives an opportunity of escaping without further loss. On the breaking out of the war of 1641, the county was overrun by the De Burgos; and though Sligo was taken from them the year after, by Sir Frederick Hamilton, it fell into their hands again, and remained in their possession until finally subdued by Ireton and Sir Charles Coote. In the war of 1688, Sligo was in the possession of the troops of James11., but they vacated it after raising the siege of Derry, through a stratagem contrived by Lieut.-Col. Gore: the forces of William 111.were, however, too much exhausted to follow up their advantage, so that the country fell again into the possession of the Irish, and the town surrendered the following year to Lord Granard. During the French invasion, in 1798, General Humbert, after the battle of Castlebar, instead of proceeding towards Dublin, turned northwards through this county in the hope of being able to co-operate with a larger force destined to act upon the north of Ireland: he was stopped at Collooney by the City of Limerick militia, commanded by Col. Vereker, afterwards Lord Gort, who though much inferior in numbers, gave him such a check as induced him to turn towards Longford, where he was surrounded by the whole of the army under the Marquess of Cornwallis, and forced to surrender at discretion.

This county is partly in the diocese of Elphin, partly in that of Killala, but chiefly in that of Achonry. For purposes of civil jurisdiction it is divided into the baronies of Carbury, Coolavin, Corran Leyny, Tirerill, and Tireragh. It contains the borough sea-port, market assize town of Sligo; the market and post towns of Ballymote and Collooney; the market town of Coolaney and the post town of Dromore West: the principal villages are Ballysadare (which has a penny post), Tubbercurry, Ardnaree, Easkey, Grange, and Riverstown. It sent four members to the Irish Parliament, two for the county and two for the borough of Sligo; since the union its representatives in the Imperial parliament have been the two members for the county at large, and one for the Borough. The election takes place in the town of Sligo. The constituency as registered to the beginning of 1837, consisted of 268 freeholders of £50, 195 of £20, and 542 of £10; 1 leaseholder of £50, 5 of £20, and 4 of £10; 4 rent chargers of £50 and 20 of £20; making a total of 1039 registered electors. The county is in the Connaught circuit: the assizes and general sessions of the peace are held in Sligo; general sessions of the peace are also held four times in the year at Ballymote and Easkey, in each of which towns there is a court-house and bridewell, but the county jail and court-house are in the town of Sligo. The district lunatic asylum is at Ballinasloe, but the greater part of the lunatics belonging to the county are kept in the county goal: the county infirmary and fever hospital are in Sligo, there are dispensaries at Ballymote, Carney, Castleconnor, Collooney, Coolaney, Dromore West, Riverstown, St John's Sligo, and Tubbercurry. The local government is vested in a lieutenant, 10 deputy lieutenants, and 83 other magistrates. There are 31 constabulary police stations, having a force of a stipendiary magistrate, a sub inspector, five chief officers, 34 constables, 120 men, and six horses. The Grand Jury presentments for 1835 amounted to £22,231. 17. 7. of which £1,382. 11. 1. was for the making and repairing of roads and bridges of the county at large; £9,167. 18. 7. for those of the baronies £6936. 8. 10. for public buildings, charities, officers salaries and incidents; £3,202.11.00 for the police; and £1,542. 8. 1.for repayment of advances made by Government. In the military arrangements, the county is included in the western district, and contains a barrack for cavalry at Sligo, affording accommodation for seven officers, 96 non-commissioned officers and men, and 60 horses.

The surface is much varied, having near the sea coast extensive plains backed by lofty mountains. The interior is hilly, with several lakes interspersed with some rivers, which, though not of great length of size, add much to the beauty of the scenery by their romantic borders and precipitous currents. The western part of the county, which stretches along the southern shore of Donegal bay, is chiefly bog, backed likewise by a range of lofty hills. Benbulben, in the north, is not more remarkable for its great elevation than from the singularity of its shape: it forms the western extremity of a range extending from Lough Erne; its northern side is nearly perpendicular; the only access to its summit, which is a table land of some extent and covered with a rich variety of plants, is by the south. Thence to the town of Sligo the country is an extensive plain richly cultivated. Knocknarea, a mountain of considerable elevation and with an extensive base, situated on the peninsula formed by the estuaries

of Sligo and Ballysadare rivers, is a very striking object in every point of view. The Ox Mountains extend along the western verge of the county into Mayo: the whole of the south is rugged and hilly, rising into the high range of the Curlews on the border of Roscommon. There are three lakes remarkable alike for size and beauty: the most northern is Lough Gill, near the town of Sligo, on the east; it is about nine miles long and three broad, studded with islands, some of which are richly wooded and others present an expanse of verdant meadow. Of these islands two only are inhabited, namely, Innismore, called also Church Island, from the remains of a monastic building, the cemetery of which is still used as a place of internment and where the incumbent of St. John's, on his presentation, still takes possession; and Cottage Island, so called from a beautiful modern lodge erected on it. Besides these, there are 16 other islands, all more or less wooded. Lough Arrow, nearly of the same size as the preceding, but more irregular in its outline, and equally beautiful for the picturesque variety of its scenery, contains the three islands of Innismore, Innisbeg, and Annaghgowla: there is fine fishing in this lake in April and May. At the most southern extremity of the county, and forming part of its boundary of the side of Roscommon, is Lough Gara, equally picturesque and irregular, and also studded with islands, the chief of which are named Derrymore, Inse, Inchymore, and Inchybeg. In the Ox mountains is Lough Talt, or the High Lake, surrounded by cliffs that seem to have been thrown up by some extraordinary convulsion of nature: the lake, which is about a mile long by half a mile in breadth, is well stocked with trout of a small size, of which it is said that, while those which feed on one side of it are peculiarly ill-flavoured and misshapen, having heads exceeding the body in size, those found in other parts are of good shape and flavour. Two rocky islets near its centre are covered during the summer months with flocks of gulls and other aquatic birds. More northwards, in the same range of mountains, is Lough Easkey. The seacoast is indented by numerous bays. Near the northern extremity is the harbour of Mullaghmore, where a pier, which has fifteen feet depth at high water, has been built at the expense of Lord Palmerston, for the accommodation of the fishermen.

This part of Lord Palmerston's estate is much injured by the spreading of the sand over the surface to the depth of several feet, which is attributed to the pulling up of the bent that grew along the shore. Further south is Milkhaven, an inlet of some extent, but difficult of access, and fit only for vessels of small draught; at its entrance is *Carrig-na-Spaniahg*, or "the Spanish rock," so called from the loss of one of the vessels of the Armada, which struck upon it. At Rinoran Point, the coast expands into Sligo bay, by an opening five miles broad to its further extremity at Aughris head. On the northern side is the elevated peninsula of Raughly, connected with the sand hills on the shore by a narrow neck of land. The bay then divides into three inlets, of which that in the middle leading to Sligo is the only one of importance, the others being rocky and nearly dry at low water: the northern from the shores of which come to Lissadell oysters, is called Drumcliffe bay; the southern is the embouchure of Ballysadare river, at the entrance of which is a very profitable turbot bank. Ballysadere river is navigable to the village, where there is as good anchorage for shipping as at Sligo: During the last three years there has been a considerable export from it of oats and oatmeal, and an import of coal. Salmon are prevented from going up this river by a ledge of rock which crosses it and forms a very fine waterfall. The passage up to Sligo, which is five miles from the coast, is tortuous and difficult; vessels of large size must lie at the mouth, as there is only ten feet of water at the quay; they are, however, well protected by Oyster island and Coney island, which form a natural breakwater at the entrance; the former of these islands has a bed of oysters of large size but inferior in flavour to those of Lissadell. South of Coney Island is Maguin's island, of small dimensions. Innismurray lies two leagues out at sea on the northern coast, rising into a precipitous cliff towards the ocean, but shelving down like steps on that towards the land: it has but one entrance, called by the inhabitants 'The Hole:' a description of it is given under its own head. From Aughris head the coast takes a western direction along a rocky shore to the opening into Killala bay, and thence to the mouth of the Moy, which forms the boundary of the county, and opens into the harbours of Ballina and Killala.

The climate is very temperate, but so variable that the best barometers are uncertain as to the indications of wet or dry weather. The whole county may be called a tillage county, although there are numerous tracts more peculiarly suited to the fattening of cattle. In the north the soil is either a thin turf moss, on a freestone gravelly bottom, or a thin sandy loam skirted with large tracts of bog. In proceeding southward the soil becomes less moory, deeper and richer. The vicinity of Sligo presents a plain of great fertility, resting on a substratum of limestone or calcareous gravel. The central baronies to the south of the town are the most fertile, being covered except where interrupted by hills, with a very rich deep soil, well suited to the growth of wheat, potatoes, and every kind of green crop. In the most southern extremity the soil changes its character with the aspect of the surface, the rocky mountain tracts being covered with a stratum of freestone gravel and rock, interspersed with land of excellent quality fit for every kind of tillage or for pasturage. In the west the soil is light and gravelly, with large tracts of black bog and moory mountain, much of which is capable of improvement, but the best land in the entire county is around Ballymote. Throughout most parts there occurs a substratum called *lac-leigh*, which is corrupted Irish for 'a grey flag;' it is found from nine to twelve inches beneath the surface, and is, when undisturbed, perfectly impervious, therefore retentive of water. Siliceous marl in a concrete state seems to be its principal ingredient. It effervesces slightly with acids, is of a leaden grey colour, and when dug up and exposed to the atmosphere, resolves into a coarse grained friable powder. Its presence would be a complete bar to the progress of tillage, were it not that experience has proved that, when dug and well incorporated with the super incumbent soil, it improves the compost, and, when broken through, the ground below consists of limestone gravel, into which the water retained by the stubborn shell is immediately absorbed. Trenching the land for potatoes breaks the stratum, and carries off the water so effectually that no other drains are necessary.

The size of farms varies from three acres and even less to 400 or 500; those of larger size were formerly held by several tenants in partnership, and consisted usually of a small portion of tillage land to which an extensive tract of coarse mountain and bottom land was annexed, but this mode of tenure is on the decline: most of the large farms are now held by one individual and consist chiefly of pasture land. Tillage has increased rapidly; the principal crops are oats and potatoes, very little wheat being sown. The rotation system and green crops are common with the gentry, and, through the laudable exertions of Mr. Cooper, and Major O'Hara, who have formed farming societies for the diffusion of agricultural knowledge, and for improvements in rural economy by means of premiums, they are gradually extending among the small farmers. A pair of horses abreast and driven by the ploughman is now often seen; a pair of asses may also be frequently seen ploughing instead of horses. Oxen were formerly used under the plough, but never at present. In the mountainous districts much of the tillage is performed by the spade or loy. Natural manures are found in the greatest abundance in every part; sea-sand, which is collected in large quantities along the coast, proves an excellent manure for potatoes, when spread some time before the seed is planted, as otherwise the potato produced by it is wet; lime, marl, and sea-weed are also used. Vast beds of oyster shells stretch along different parts of the shore, and are even found in the interior, at some miles from the coast, at an elevation of 60 feet above high water mark; they make the best manure; even the sand in which they are imbedded is so impregnated with calcareous particles as to be used beneficially for the same purpose. The fences in some parts are broad ditches faced with stone or sods, and sometimes planted with quicksets; in others they are dry stone walls which give a denuded and sterile appearance to the parts in which they are used. The soil is peculiarly adapted to pasturage; the rich low lands fatten bullocks of the largest size for the Dublin and English markets. On the hilly districts towards the west, sheep are grazed in large flocks, and on those in the interior herds of young cattle are reared. On some of the mountains the sheep and horses are subject to a disease called the staggers, that often proves fatal, yet horned cattle feeding on the same pasture are never subject to it. Near Ardnaree cattle are affected with a disease called "crasson," in every apparent symptom similar to the gout; in the early stage of the complaint, feeding with hot bran has proved an infallible remedy.

The favourite breed of cattle is a cross between the Durham and the native cow; that between the long-horned Leicester and the native is also much esteemed; equal attention is paid to the breed of sheep. Around Sligo and Ballymote are some excellent dairy farms, and butter is made by all the small farmers, by much the greater part of which is shipped at Sligo for the British market. Good horses are brought from Galway and Roscommon; the native breed is small, light, and unsightly. Pigs are numerous, of large size and very profitable. Goats, which are sometimes seen on the small farms and near the mountains, are of small size and by no means numerous. The land indicates a strong tendency to produce timber spontaneously: the escars are generally covered with brushwood; and even among the clefts of the rocks in the mountain glens the oak, hazel, yew, holly, and beech shoot forth, requiring only protection from the inroads of cattle to come to maturity. Around the mansions of the gentry there are large and thriving plantations; planting forest trees in hedgerows is becoming every year more customary. The only trees that thrive near the coast are the sycamore and the willow, whose pliancy allows them to give way under the pressure of the blasts from the Atlantic. Alder also flourishes for a time in these exposed situations, but soon decays. The arbutus grows spontaneously, but does not attain the same size as in the south-western counties. Myrtle is to be seen in great abundance in sheltered situations.

The county forms the north-western extremity of the great central floetz limestone field of Ireland, interrupted in two places by the mica slate formation, one to the south of Lough Gill, the other along the western mountain range, which in its utmost extent stretches from Foxford in Mayo, by Collooney, to Manorhamilton in Leitrim. This range is very narrow, seldom exceeding three miles and at Collooney being less than a quarter of a mile in breadth. It is generally succeeded by beds of red or yellowish sandstone or by limestone. The sandstone formation is of very unequal thickness and irregular in its arrangement, in some places rising into mountains, in others not exceeding 20 or 30 feet in height: it is sometimes, though rarely, interstratified with red or grey sandstone slate, in which case its resemblance to that of the coal formation has led to expensive and illusory attempts to obtain this valuable mineral. Iron-ore is abundant in many places, particularly at Ballintogher and at the base of the Ox mountains. Near Screevenamuck are extensive excavations whence the ore was raised as long as timber could be procured to make charcoal for smelting it: the last furnace was extinguished in 1768. Lead-ore has been found in several parts of the limestone district, and worked for some time feebly and unprofitably. A silver mine, which produced some specimens of very pure metal, was worked near Ballysadare. Iron pyrites and sulphate of copper are often found in small detached pieces, and some pure specimens of the latter metal were found in the Owenmore and Collooney rivers; black oxide of manganese is often seen on the surface and very large pieces of the ore have been found in several parts. At the foot of some of the mountains, and in the beds of some rivers, carbonate of copper and various kinds of ochre, all indicative of extensive mineral deposits, have been discovered: as also very large and beautiful amethysts in the neighbourhood of Ballymote.

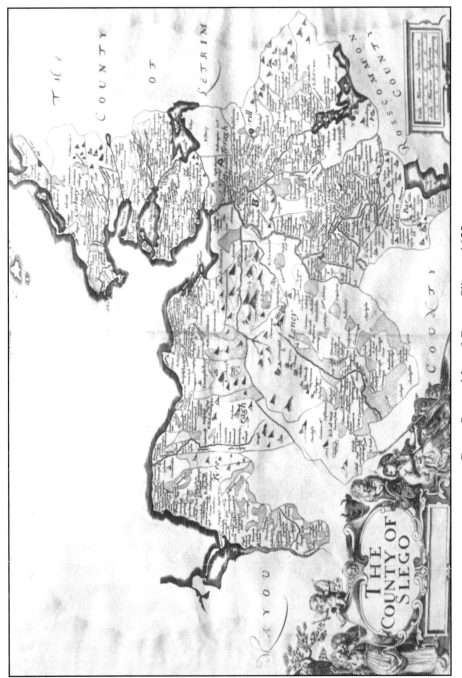

Down Survey Map of County Sligo c. 1655.

The linen manufacture was introduced into Sligo by the spirited exertions of Lord Shelburne, who, in 1749, brought thither a colony of weavers and settled them on his estate at Ballymote, then a thinly inhabited and almost uncultivated waste, whose population was employed solely in the herding of cattle. The death of this nobleman for a time checked the progress of the manufacture, but it revived under the guidance of Mr. Fitzmaurice who, on succeeding to the estate, after having made himself practically acquainted with all the processes of the trade, superintended the establishment in person, and thus powerfully stimulated those engaged in it. Each weaver was provided with a cottage, half a rood of land for a potato garden, and grass for a cow, thus affording him the means of subsistence for his family without allowing his time or thoughts to be distracted from his main business by the details of a small farm. This well-devised exertion gave a turn to the public mind throughout the country, and led to the establishment of the manufacture on a general scale, which flourished for many years. The manufacture of unions, a mixed fabric of linen and cotton, has been introduced and is carried on extensively. Mr. Fitzmaurice also encouraged the erection of bleach-greens upon a large scale, and having built very extensive bleach-works near the town of Denbigh, in North Wales, he purchased the brown linens in every market of Sligo and the adjoining counties, and thus greatly benefited both Wales and Ireland. The linen trade is still the staple of the county, and though by no means so prosperous or extensive as formerly, a brisk trade in it is still carried on: there are four bleach-greens in full operation, finishing nearly 40,000 pieces annually, which are principally shipped for England and generally destined for the American markets. Coarse woollen cloths and friezes are made for domestic use, and a very extensive trade is carried on in the purchase of flannels, druggets, stockings and other fabrics of Connaught manufacture. Merchants from many parts of Ireland, but particularly from Ulster, come to Sligo to meet the Connaught factors. The only other branches of trade, except as connected with the port of Sligo, are tanning, distilling, and brewing. Kelp is made around the greater part of the coast but since the reduction of the duty on barilla, this source of employment has declined considerably, and by much the greater portion of the plant now collected is used as manure, being dried by the peasantry near the shore, by whom it is sold to the farmers of the interior, who draw it home to distances of 20 miles and upwards. Fish is taken in large quantities off the coast, of which cod, haddock, and turbot are the most abundant kinds, except herrings, which appear here in vast shoals; but as the boats and nets are badly constructed and very incomplete in their equipment, little advantage is taken of this productive source of wealth. Sprats are also taken in great quantities; indeed this is the only kind of fishing for which either the boats or tackle are adapted. Oysters of excellent flavour are found in several beds; those of Lissadell are the most sought after; great numbers are sent to Dublin, where they are sometimes more highly esteemed than even the Carlingford oysters. A very extensive and profitable salmon fishery is carried on at Ballina, on the river Moy, which separates this county from Mayo; there is another very valuable fishery at the town of Sligo, and others of minor importance in some of the smaller inlets.

The rivers of the county are few, and short in their course, but generally rapid; that which flows from Lough Gill is usually called the Sligo river, from its passing through the town, but its proper name is the Garavogue. The water of Ballysadare, also thus named from the town, but properly called the Unshin, is formed by the river Arrow, which flows from the lake of that name and forms a junction with the Owenmore and the Owenbeg, near the town of Collooney; the united waters form the first-named river, and flowing northward to Ballysadare, over a succession of cascades, form the greater horn of Sligo bay. The river Moy rises in the Ox mountains and flows nearly south, through the barony of Leney, where it enters the county of Mayo, flowing westward through the barony of Gallen, and shortly after turning due north it meets the waters of Loughs Conn and Cullen; thence it proceeds by Foxford to Ardmore, where it becomes the boundary between Sligo and Mayo; thence by Ballina, Rosserick Abbey, and Moyne, to the sea, where it opens into the spacious bay of Killala. The entrance of the Moy, which had been impassable for vessels of any size in consequence of the bar at its mouth, has been rendered navigable for ships of large burden, which can now come up to the town of Ballina; this important improvement is chiefly owing to the exertions of John Levington, Esq., a merchant in the town. The Easkey rises in Lough Eask between the Ox mountains and Knocknaree, and flows due north to the sea parallel with the Moy. There are many smaller rivers and streams, particularly among the mountains, all tributary to one of those above mentioned. The roads are numerous in the eastern part of the county, and generally well laid out and in good order. A new line, lately completed between Ballysadare and Ballina, through the western baronies into Mayo, must prove of incalculable advantage, by facilitating the communication between the two counties, and affording a vent for the produce of the district it traverses, which was hitherto nearly unprofitable for want of such an outlet. The road is constructed on the most scientific principles.

At Drumcliffe are the remains of a round tower of coarser construction and smaller dimensions than any other now known; it is considerably injured by time: at the same place are two stone crosses, one in a perfect state, the other much mutilated and decayed. About two miles from Sligo, on the Dublin road, the ground is overspread to a great extent with druidical circles, called, by the peasantry, Giants' Graves; one of them, called *Lugna Clogh*, is a cromlech of large stones, under which human bones have been found. The names of Giants' houses has been given to a number of grottos hollowed out of the west side of the hill or rock of Corran, to which access is obtained only by a steep and very difficult entrance: their origin or use has not been satisfactorily ascertained. About a mile from Castleconnor several vaulted square rooms have been discovered, built of large stones and communicating with each other by an exterior circular passage; in the centre is a cavity unconnected with any of the other chambers; it is conjectured to have been either a granary or a cemetery of the Ostmen. On Inishmurray island are some small chapels of great antiquity, in one of which is a rudely sculptured statue of wood, said to represent St. Molaise, the patron; these relics are more particularly described in the account of the island, *which see*. A circular stone fort, called

Knockamoyle Skreen, stands on the summit of a high hill near Skreen church. Many cairns and remains of what seem to have been places of defence are visible on Knocknarea mountain. The vestiges of monastic institutions are very numerous: the ruins of those of Ballysadare, Ballindoon, Ballinlig, Ballymote, Banada, Cloonameehan, Court, Inishmore, Inishmurray and Sligo, are still remaining; some of them are large and very handsome; those of Billa, Drumcliffe, Drumcolumb, Drumrat, Killaraght, Kilmacowen, Kilnamanagh, and Skreen have been converted into parish churches; those of Achonry, Agharois, Akeras, Ardnary, Ardseinlis, Athmoy, Caille, Caillevinde, Cashel, Craoghgrellain, Druimederdalogh, Druimlias, Druimna, Echenach or Enaceich, Emlyfadd, Enachaird, Glendallain, Kilchairpre, Killuathren, Kilrasse, Knockmore, Snamluther, and Templehouse are known only by name, In the yard which surrounds the church of Kilmacteige, near Banada,, are the ruins of an ancient building, said to have been a college, but no particulars of its history are known. The principal ancient castles, all more or less in ruins, are those of Ardnaglass, Behy, Ballyhara, Ballymote, Ballinafad, Castleconnor, Enniscrone, Lackan, Meemlough, Newtown, Moygara, Rathlee, Roselee, Sligo, and Tanrego. The modern residences of the gentry, which are very numerous and in many instances highly ornamental, are more particularly noticed in their respective parishes.

The habitations of the peasantry are very mean but progressively improving: the walls are sometimes of stone, but more generally of sods, roofed with sticks and thatched with heath and straw, or rushes, in alternate layers. The fuel is turf: the use of coal brought from England, Wales, and Scotland, in trading vessels which return laden with grain, is confined to the town of Sligo and its vicinity. The food is potatoes with an occasional admixture of oaten bread, milk, eggs, fresh or salted herrings and other sea-fish. The clothing is chiefly home-made frieze. The women are dressed in stuffs and druggets of domestic manufacture; cottons for upper garments are now much worn, and few are to be seen without stockings and shoes, at least on Sundays and holidays. The English language is generally spoken through every part of the county, but elderly people in the mountainous districts still speak Irish. A striking difference is perceptible between the population here and that of the northern counties: the former is a much more diminutive race, and the character of the countenance indicates a different origin. Early marriages are encouraged, and the ceremony is attended with much expense: the favourite season for marrying is from Christmas to Lent, being that least occupied in agriculture. The disputes arising at fairs or markets or in their dealings with each other, were frequently and are still occasionally decided by arbitration before persons chosen by the parties at variance: these judges are called Brehons, and are generally recompensed for the loss of time devoted to hearing the cause by being regaled with whiskey at the expense of the parties; but these customs are falling into disuse, and most of the disputes are now taken to the petty or quarter sessions. Attendance on the wakes of deceased friends and neighbours is another source of expense. The estimation in which a man has been held during life is judged of by the attendance on these occasions and at his funeral: to be absent is therefore considered a serious offence, and much expense is incurred in procuring the necessary refreshments for the numbers that attend. Although this ancient custom of waking the corpse and attending the funeral is still kept up, the Irish cry or howl is now rarely heard. In the mountain parish of Kilmacteige there is a tract of country which for several years has scarcely ever been free from a low malignant typhus fever, of which great numbers die after a lingering illness of fifteen or twenty days: the cause is attributed to the moist and chilly nature of the soil, and not any peculiarity in the dietetics of the people. In the same parish are two wells much resorted to for devotional purposes: one of them, called Tubber Art, is celebrated for its efficacy in restoring to health persons whose cases had proved hopeless under the ordinary modes of treatment. In a rock near the entrance to the old church in Innismore, or Church Island, in Lough Gill, is a cavity called 'My Lady's Bed,' in which women who lie down and repeat certain formulary believe themselves to be secured from the peril of death in childbed. Among the natural curiosities may be mentioned a singular peculiarity in a stream in Glenduff, in which, when the wind blows strong from the south-west, at every gust the stream, which flows perpendicularly down the mountain, is divided into two, and one part flows to the bottom, while the other is carried back up the mountain, and as long as the gust continues the channel of the stream is quite dry. At the base of Knocknarea mountain is a chasm, commonly called 'The Glen', apparently formed by some violent convulsion of nature: it is about a mile long, of considerable breadth and depth, in several parts well furnished with trees and enlivened by small cascades. Sulphureous and chalybeate springs are found among the mountains of Tireragh, where also the common spring and river waters are peculiarly pure and pellucid. This county gives the title of Marquess to the family of Browne.

BOROUGH OF SLIGO

Seal

Sligo, a sea-port, assize, borough, market and post-town, in the barony of Carbury, 103 miles (N. W.) from Dublin; containing 15,152 inhabitants. This place, which is the chief town of the county, is indebted for its importance to one of the first English settlers in Ireland. So early as 1245, a castle was erected here by Maurice Fitzgerald, Earl of Kildare, and at the time Lord Justice of Ireland. The same Earl, in 1252, founded also a monastery, which he dedicated to the Holy Cross, for friars of the order of St. Dominick, the origin of which establishment has by some writers been erroneously ascribed to O'Conor Sligo.

In 1270 the town and the castle were destroyed by O'Donnell; but the monastery escaped the ravages of that chieftain, and the castle afterwards rebuilt by Richard, Earl of Ulster, in 1310. In 1360 the town was again destroyed by fire, and in 1394 it was plundered and burnt by Mac William Burgh. In 1414 the monastery was wholly consumed by an accidental fire, and for its restoration Pope John XX11. granted indulgences to all who should visit it and contribute towards the expense of rebuilding it. In 1416 it was rebuilt by Bryan Mac Dermot Mac Donagh, sole monarch of Tír Ollioll (now the barony of Tirerill), who in 1454, was interred within its walls. It continued to flourish till the dissolution, when it was granted to Sir William Taaffe. At the commencement of the reign of Jas. 1., a grant of market and two annual fairs to be held here was made by Sir Jas. Fullerton; and in 1613 the Town was made a Parliamentary Borough by charter of incorporation. In 1621, it received a charter of staple, incorporating a mayor, two constables and merchants, with the same powers as those of Youghal. In 1627 Sir James Craig had a fresh grant of a market and two fairs, which in 1674 were granted to William, Earl of Strafford, and Thomas Radcliffe, Esq. In the war of 1641 the town was taken without opposition by Sir Chas. Coote, at the head an army of 4000 infantry and 500 horse. By his occupation of this post, Sir Charles had the means of keeping a check upon the royalists of the neighbouring counties; but the R.C. Archbishop of Tuam with great zeal collected forces for the recovery of the town, in which

attempt he was joined by Sir Jas. Dillon, who was sent by the Confederates in Kilkenny with 800 men to his assistance, and having forced his way into the town was on the point of expelling the Parliamentarians, when he was suddenly alarmed by the intelligence of an army being on its approach to their relief. Upon this the confederated forces retired, and in their retreat were attacked and routed by Sir Chas. Coote; the archbishop was killed in the action, and among his papers were found the important documents that exposed the connection of the King with the Catholic party. The Parliamentarians afterwards abandoned the town, which, though threatened again by Sir Chas. Coote on his advance against Limerick, in 1651, was retained by the Catholics till the termination of the war. In the war of the revolution it was taken by the brave Enniskilliners, who also defeated a large body of James's forces that were advancing against it, and took from them a considerable booty; but the garrison was shortly after driven out by Gen. Sarsfield, and the place was finally reduced by the Earl of Granard.

The town is now the property chiefly of Lord Palmerston and Owen Wynne, of Hazelwood, Esq. It is advantageously situated on the banks of the river Garavogue, which connects Lough Gill with the bay of Sligo, opening to the Atlantic; the river is about two miles and a half in length and the town is situated on the extremity of it nearest to the sea, where it is narrowest. This river is navigable from Lough Gill to the town; but a weir across prevents the navigation thence to the sea, to the great injury of the commercial interests of the place. The greater portion of the town is on the south side of the river, in the parish of St. John, and is connected with the smaller portion, in the parish of Calry, on the north side, by two bridges. The streets are irregularly formed, which detracts much from its internal appearance, though the houses are chiefly of respectable character, and there are several of a superior order; as seen, however, in combination with the surrounding scenery, it forms an interesting and pleasing feature in the landscape from many points of view in the vicinity. The total number of houses is 2,238. It is lighted and paved under a local Act of the 43rd of Geo. 111., the provision of which are stated in the subsequent account of the corporation. The inhabitants are supplied with water from public pumps, kept in repair by the Commissioners appointed under the above-named act. A public library and two reading-rooms are supported by subscription; and a newspaper is published every Saturday. There is a small theatre, which is very irregularly attended; races are generally held annually in August on the race-course of Bomore, about five miles from the town; and a regatta is held on Lough Gill, which is very numerously attended. The barracks for cavalry are capable of accommodating 7 officers and 96 non-commissioned officers and privates, with stabling for 60 horses; an excellent hospital for 15 patients is annexed to them. There are a few linen and stocking weavers, who work on their own account, but no large factories; the linen trade, formerly carried on here to some extent, has almost ceased, and the linen-hall is unoccupied. A distillery, belonging to Messrs Martin, Madden and Co., manufactures 120,000 gallons of whiskey annually and affords employment to 55 persons. There are four breweries, and several manufactories for soap, candles, snuff, tobacco, hats, ropes and cables; also several extensive flour-mills.

Sligo Abbey, founded by Maurice Fitzgerald in 1252 for the Dominican Order, was accidentally burned to the ground in 1414, but was afterwards restored through the exertions of the Prior, Bryan McDonagh. It was abandoned in 1698. Architecturally, it is a fine example of the workmanship of that era, particularly the cloisters. This ancient edifice is the oldes link with Sligo's storied past.

The trade is facilitated by the river, which is navigable through Lough Gill and supplies the town with turf and other necessaries. The maritime trade of the port is the chief source of the prosperity of the town, and its rapid increase may be ascertained from the fact that, in the year 1800, the number of vessels that entered the port was 65, of the aggregate burden of 4,100 tons; while in the year 1830, the number of vessels was 540, and the aggregate burden, 57,016 tons. In 1834, 47 vessels in the foreign trade entered inwards and 2 cleared outwards, and 354 in the coasting and cross-channel trade entered inwards and 508 cleared outwards; there were 17 vessels belonging to the port that year. The principal exports are corn, butter and provisions; and the chief import, timber, salt and every article of West India produce, which are distributed over a very large tract of country, this being the only port of importance between Londonderry and Galway. The amount of duties paid at the custom-house, in 1826, was £33,565; in 1830, £36,325; and in 1836, £35,864. The amount of excise duties collected in the revenue district of which this town is the head, for 1835, was £44,180. The custom-house and the King's warehouses, which are the property of the crown, are well adapted to the purposes for which they were built; and the quays, which are very commodious, and are kept in good repair by the commissioners, have a depth of water 12 feet at spring tides, which will allow vessels of 300 tonnes burden to moor close to them. Many emigrants from this and the neighbouring counties sail hence annually for America. The principal markets are on Tuesday and Saturday for provisions and agricultural produce; they are well attended. A market for corn and another for butter are opened daily in buildings erected for them by Owen Wynne, Esq. Fairs, chiefly for cattle, are held on the 27th March, the Saturday after the 1st May (O.S.), 4th July, 12th August and the 9th of October. There is a large salmon fishery on the river, with which is connected a pond, the property of Abraham Martin, Esq., so constructed that the fish can easily enter but cannot quit it, by which means there is a supply of fresh salmon at all times. A chief constabulary police station has been established here; and it is also the residence of the inspecting commander of the Sligo coast-guard district, which comprises the five subordinate stations of Enniscrone, Pullocheny,

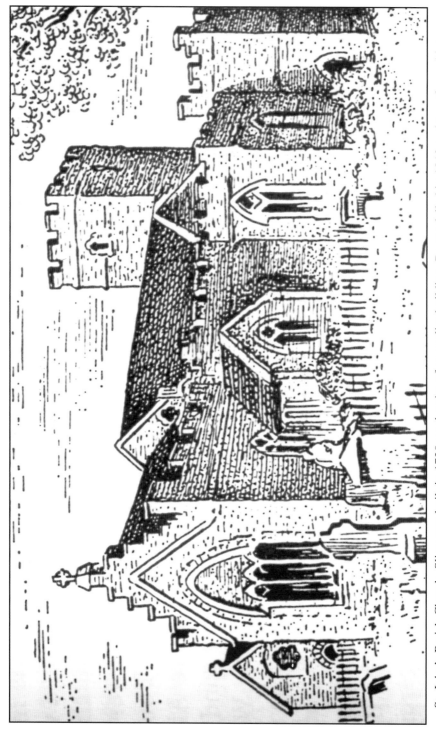

St. John's Parish Church, Sligo was built in 1730 on the site of an earlier building. Re-modelled in 1812 and transformed into a Gothic structure. It is now the Cathedral Church of the diocese of Elphin and Ardagh

Pullindiva, Raughly and Mullaghmore.

Sligo bay is situated between Aughris Head and Rinoran Point; it is about five miles in breadth at the mouth, and extends as much inland; the upper part divides into three inlets, of which the central one only, leading to the town, is of importance, as each of the others has a bar and is nearly dry at low water. On the north side is Raughly, a small peninsula of rising ground, connected by a low narrow neck, with some sand hills on the shore at its south-west side is the Wheaten Rock, extending nearly half a mile N.E. and S.W., and partly dry at spring tides. At the south end of Raughly, about two cables' length off the shore, are the Bird rocks; about half a mile to the eastward a vessel may lie in moderate weather in 2 fathoms, and there is a small pier with 12 feet of water inside the point. At the distance of one mile south from Raughly is the point of the reef called the Black rock, extending to the north end of Coney Island, having the western part entirely and the rest nearly dry a low water; a lighthouse has been erected on it, and channel into Sligo lies close along its north side; shallows from this point towards Lissadell form the bar of Sligo, on which are only 10 feet at low water. Ships drawing 12 feet of water should take half flood into the harbour, for with westerly winds there is generally a heavy sea between Raughly and the point of Ross. Two lighthouses have been erected on Oyster Island.

By a charter dated the 20th March, 11th of Jas. 1., the town was incorporated under the name of the "Provost and free Burgesses, of the Borough of Sligo;"the corporate body to consist of a provost, twelve free burgesses, and a commonalty. The provost, who is elected annually, is judge of the Borough court, which is a court of record with civil jurisdiction to the amount of £3. 6. 8., and still continues to be held weekly; he is also clerk of the market. The burgesses are elected for life by the provost and other burgesses. Usage, confirmed by a judgement of the court of King's bench, has given the right of admission to the freedom wholly to the provost and burgesses. The charter also constitutes the corporation a guild mercatory: the subordinate officers are a town-clerk and recorder, a weigh master and two sergeants-at-mace. A charter granted by Jas. 11., in the 4th year of his reign, has

Phillips' *Prospect of Sligo*, 1685, showing the Stone Fort (left): The Abbey (centre); and the Green Fort (top right).

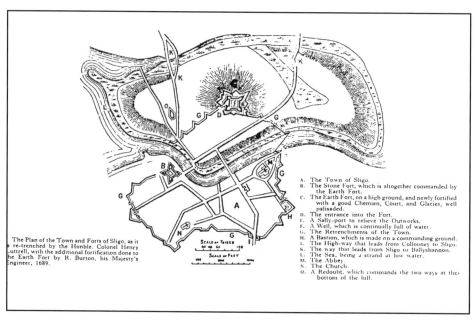

The Plan of the Town and Forts of Sligo, as it re-trenched by the Honble. Colonel Henry Luttrell, with the additional fortification done to he Earth Fort by R. Burton, his Majesty's Engineer, 1689.

A. The Town of Sligo.
B. The Stone Fort, which is altogether commanded by the Earth Fort.
C. The Earth Fort, on a high ground, and newly fortified with a good Chemien, Court, and Glacies, well palisaded.
D. The entrance into the Fort.
E. A Sally-port to relieve the Outworks.
F. A Well, which is continually full of water.
G. The Retrenchments of the Town.
H. A Bastion, which is made on a commanding ground.
I. The High-way that leads from Collooney to Sligo.
K. The way that leads from Sligo to Ballyshannon.
L. The Sea, being a strand at low water.
M. The Abbey.
N. The Church.
O. A Redoubt, which commands the two ways at their bottom of the hill.

A plan of the fortications of Sligo Town, 1689, during the Williamite Wars, showing the Green Fort (top centre) and an outline of the street formation of that era.

not been acted upon. By a local act of the 30th of Geo. 11., c. 21, it was directed that the corporation should be conservators of the port and should maintain a ballast-office; and subsequently, by an act of the 40th of Geo. 111., c. 49, for the management of the concerns of the town, amended by another of the 43rd of Geo. 111., c. 60, commissioners were appointed, consisting of the representatives of the county and borough, the provost and burgesses, and 24 others, resident in the town or within five miles of it, and to be elected by holders of houses of the yearly value of £20, who are empowered to regulate the paving, flagging, lighting, watching and improving the town, to regulate the markets, and also the carriages and porters; to improve the quays and to make and repair the docks and wharfs; to improve the port and harbour, to regulate the pilotage, and to assess taxes at a minimum of 2s. 6d. in the pound on all houses of the annual value of £5 and upwards, for defraying the expenses incurred in the execution of these duties. The commissioners are also empowered to raise a fund for these purposes to the amount of £2,000 for the town, and £6,000 for the harbour. The boundary of their jurisdiction is fixed at the distance of a mile from the market cross in every direction. By letters patent of Chas. 11., in the 27th of his reign, the town and certain lands were erected into the manor of Sligo, with a court baron with civil jurisdiction to the amount of 40s., and a court of record with civil jurisdiction to the amount of £100 and a court leet to be held before the seneschal; no manor courts are now held.

The only property belonging to the corporation consists of about 19 acres of land, which was formerly a common, let at £98. 3. 8. per annum; and a plot of a rood of ground, formerly a pound, but now built upon, let at £10 per annum. The charter also conferred upon the provost and burgesses the privilege of returning two members to the Irish parliament, which they exercised till the Union, since which time they have returned one member only to the Imperial parliament. The right of election, previously vested in the corporation, has by the recent act, for amending the representation, been extended to the £10 householders within the borough, the limits of which are the same as those defined by acts for the purpose of local taxation already

The armorial altar tomb of the O'Connor family in Sligo Abbey, 1624, containing the shield and crest of the O'Connors flanked by two figures representing St. Peter and St. Paul. In the centre compartment is a representation of Donough O'Connor and his wife Eleanor Butler kneeling in prayer. In the surrounds are numerous trophies including drum, flax, axe, shield and sword.

referred to. The provost is the returning officer. The assizes and the general sessions of the peace for the county are held here, the latter four times in the year. Petty sessions for the division are also held every Thursday. The court-house, though a spacious and well-arranged building, to which are attached the public offices, is too limited for the public business. The county goal is a handsome and substantial building, erected on the polygonal plan at the expense of £30.000; the governor's house is in the centre, and the debtors' ward and the hospital form two advanced wings; it is well adapted to the classification of the prisoners, each of whom has a separate sleeping cell; it has a tread-mill for hard labour, a school, and a surgery and dispensary within its walls; and all its departments are under excellent regulations, and it is in high repute for discipline and good order.

The Borough comprises the greater part of the parish of St. John and part of the parish of Calry, the former on the south, and the latter on the north side of the river. The patronage of the parish of St. John has been lately given to Trinity College, Dublin, the Provost and Senior Fellows of which will present the next and all the succeeding incumbents. The soil is fertile, the lands generally in a good state of cultivation, and the system of agriculture much improved. The scenery is pleasingly diversified and in many parts beautifully picturesque; the view of the town at the head of the bay, environed by mountains and embosomed in a richly cultivated country, is strikingly romantic, especially in the approach from Dromahaire. On the road from Manorhamilton is a point where, emerging from the mountains, a spacious and magnificent scene, embracing the whole of the town with its surrounding district, opens at once on the view. The approach to Sligo by the Dublin road is also very beautiful, having Lough Gill and Hazelwood demesne on the east; the bay of Sligo, with its two bold headlands of Benbulben and Knocknarea on the west; and in the centre the highly picturesque town of Sligo. Among the various residences that embellish the neighbourhood the most conspicuous is Hazelwood, the seat of Owen Wynne, Esq., a noble mansion, situated on a peninsula stretching into Lough Gill, and surrounded by a richly wooded demesne, commanding beautiful views over the lake and its wooded islands, terminated by the mountains which rise from its shores on the south. Adjoining Hazelwood is the beautiful demesne of Hollywell, lately the residence of the Hon. and Rev. Jos. Butler, brother of Lord Carrick and rector of Dromahaire. There are also in the vicinity of the town the following seats besides those noticed in the accounts of the parishes of St. John and Calry, *which see*: Cregg, the seat of the Hon. Robert King; Lissadell, of Sir Robert Gore-Booth, Bart.: Kevinsfort of G. Dodwell, Esq.; Primrose Grange, of G.D. Meredith, Esq.: Glen House,of M. Walsh, Esq.; Rathcarrick, of Roger Walker, Esq; Cloverhill of W. E. Chambers, Esq; Ballyglass, of Gowan Gilmore, Esq.; Millbrook, of J. C. Simpson, Esq.; Seafield, of W. Phibbs, Esq.: Moneygold, of J. Soden, Esq.; Ballytivnan House, of H. Griffith Esq.; Grange, of the Rev. C. West; Cairnsfoot, of Major Bromhead; Belleville, of F. O'Beirne, Esq.; Dunally, of W. Parke, Esq.; Colga, of Travers Homan, Esq.; Seamount, of Jeremy Jones, Esq.; Thornhill, of Lieut. H. J. Clifford, R. N.; Farmhill, of Dr. Walker; and Ballyweelin of H. Bolton, Esq.; The neighbourhood is resorted to as a bathing-place, but not to any great extent.

The church of St. John's parish is an old cruciform building, in excellent repair, in the later style of English architecture, with a massive square tower at the west end. The glebe-house is situated on the glebe of one acre close to the church. The church of Calry, which is also in the town, is a respectable building in the Gothic style, with a well-proportioned spire; it was erected in 1822, at the expense of £3,000, in which is included the expense of the erection of a house, offices and garden-wall for the perpetual curate, whose appointment belongs to the vicar of St. John's. The R.C. chapel of the parish of St. John's is a structure of spacious dimensions; and there is also in the town a small Dominican convent, with a chapel attached to it . There are places of worship for Presbyterians in connection with the synod of Ulster (of the third class), Independents and Wesleyan Methodists in connection with the Established Church. St John's parochial school is supported by the incumbent and the proceeds of charity sermons; a school for children of both sexes is supported in connection with the national board of education; a school is also supported by the trustees of Erasmus Smith's charity and the

Incorporated Society, the St John's female school, in which a large Sunday school is also held, is supported by subscription; and there is a female school in the parish of Calry.

The county infirmary is a handsome building of hewn limestone, erected in 1819 at an expense of £3500. It contains six wards for 30 patients, with officers' apartments and every other requisite. The fever hospital is a well arranged and handsome structure in an airy and healthful situation on the summit of a hill; it contains eight wards, and has a dispensary attached to it: these three institutions are within the same enclosure; there is also a dispensary in the parish of St John. A mendicity association is supported by private subscriptions and donations. There are some remains of the beautiful and spacious monastery of Sligo, serving to convey some idea of it's former magnificence: they consist of three sides of the cloisters, with a finely vaulted roof, and are separated from the quadrangle by a long series of pillars, of which several are sculptured and of pointed arches, in the early English style of architecture. The great east window of the church is of beautiful design and highly enriched with tracery, the high altar, which is embellished with sculpture in relief, is almost hidden by the accumulation of disinterred bones ; the nave is spacious, and the roof is supported by ranges of pillars at intervals of four feet from each other; the central tower is complete, with the exception only of the battlements; to the right of the high altar is the tomb of O'Conor, with the effigies of himself and his lady, and there are numerous vaults and cells.

Newspaper device, used as a seal in the Corporation books of Sligo.

COUNTY OF SLIGO

ACLARE a village in the parish of Kilmacteigue, 9 miles (N.E.) from Foxford, on the road to Ballymote; containing about 20 houses and 110 inhabitants. It has a market on Saturday, and is a station of the constabulary police.

AHAMLISH, a parish, in the barony of Carbury, 9 miles (N.N.W.) from Sligo, containing, with the villages of Ballintemple and Grange, and the islands Innishmurry and Dernish (which are separately described), 7,483 inhabitants. It is situated on the north-west coast, near the entrance to the bay of Sligo, and on the road from Sligo to Ballyshannon; and comprises 9,286 statute acres, of which 6,509 are applotted under the tithe act, and of which, also 7,311 are arable and pasture, and 1,975 bog and waste. The surface is naked and unadorned, having only one small wood on the lands of Grellagh, near the river Bunduff, the estate of Viscount Palmerston, who is proprietor of the greater part of the parish. The mountain of Benbulben extends in a direction of east to west, and separates this parish from Drumcliffe. The principal village is Grange, consisting of one street, in which are only four decent houses, and

the rest are thatched cabins. Some improvement in the mode of tillage has taken place of late years, but the system of husbandry is comparatively still very deficient, and the farming implements are of a very inferior kind: limestone and turf are plentiful. A great extent of bog has been reclaimed by Lord Palmerston, who has also planted large scopes of sandy banks with bent. Considerable improvements at Mullaghmore have been made exclusively by the direction and at the expense of the nobleman, which are notice under the head of that place. There is a salmon fishery in the river Bunduff; and at Mullaghmore several boats were formerly employed in taking turbot, cod, and other kinds of fish, which abound on this part of the coast. There are some corn-mills in the parish. The principal seats are Moneygold, the residence of J. Soden, Esq.; Streeda, of Booth Jones, Esq.; Grange, of the Rev. C. West, the incumbent; and Creevymore, of the Rev. J. McHugh, P.P. Seven fairs for live stock are held at Grange, and a fair on Feb. 1st is held at Cliffoney, which is also a penny post from Sligo. Grange is both a coast guard and a constabulary police station. The living is a vicarage, in the diocese of Elphin, and in the patronage of the Bishop; the rectory is impropriated in Lord Palmerston. The tithes amount to £221. 10.9., divided in moieties between the impropriator and the incumbent. The church is a plain edifice, built in 1813, for which the late Board of First Fruits granted a loan of £700, and Lord Palmerston contributed £100: it contains a marble monument to the Soden family, with an inscription recording the death of James Soden, in 1705, at the age of 109 years: the Ecclesiastical Commissioners have lately granted £119 for its repair. There is neither glebe nor glebe-house. The R.C. parish is co-extensive with that of the Established church: there are two chapels, situated at Grange and Cliffoney, and built at the sole expense of Lord Palmerston. Three schools are supported principally by his lordship, each of which has a house and garden, and in which are 170 boys and more than 100 girls; and in other private schools are taught more than 100 boys and 60 girls.

AUGHANAGH, or Aghanagh, a parish, in the barony of Tirerill, 5 miles (N.W.) from Boyle, on Lough Arrow, and on the road from Boyle to Sligo; containing 2,393 inhabitants. It is bounded on the south by the Curlew Mountains, and comprises 5,412 statute acres, as applotted under the tithe act, with a considerable extent of mountain and bog. There are quarries of excellent limestone resembling marble, and much used for building. Hollybrook, the residence of J. Folliott, Esq., is beautifully situated on the shore of Lough Arrow; the grounds are well planted, and contribute in a pleasing manner to embellish the scenery of the lake. It is a vicarage, in the diocese of Elphin, forming part of the union of Boyle: the tithes amount to £110. 15.4, of which £62. 6.1. is payable to the impropriators, and £48. 9.3. to the vicar. In the R.C. divisions it is included in the union or district of Riverstown: the chapel at Greyfort is a good slated building. At Corradoo there is a school under the patronage of Wm. Phibbs, Esq; and there is a private pay school in the parish. On the lands of Aughanagh are the remains of an Abbey.

BALLINAFAD, a village, in the parish of Aughanagh, 2 miles (N.N.W.) from Boyle, on the road to Sligo; containing 20 houses and 140 inhabitants. A fair is held on the 29th of August; and here is a station of the constabulary police. – See AUGHANAGH.

Ballinafad Castle, known as the 'Castle of the Curlews' was built in the 17th century by Captain John St. St. Barbe, who received large grants of land in the vicinity from James I

BALLINAKILL, a parish, in the barony of Tirerill, 9 miles (S.S.E.) from Sligo, containing 1,767 inhabitants. The parish is situated on the road from Sligo to Ballyfarnon, and is intersected by the small river Dubhglass, which at Rockbrook forms several small cascades, and passes under a natural bridge of one arch, 6 feet high and 20 feet in the span. It comprises 2,679 statute acres, as applotted under the tithe act; the land is good, and is chiefly under the old unimproved system of tillage; there is a large extent of bog, and limestone abounds in the parish. Rockbrook is the residence of E.H. Cogan, Esq., and Moorfield, of T. Irwin, Esq. Petty sessions are held at Sooey every third Tuesday. It is a vicarage, in the diocese of Elphin, and forms part of the union of Boyle; the rectory is appropriate to the prebend of Kilmacallan in the cathedral of Elphin. The tithes amount to £83. 1.6., payable in moieties to the prebendary and the vicar. The Protestant inhabitants resort to the church in the parish of Ballysumaghan. In the R.C. divisions it is the head of union or district, called Sooey, which comprises also the parishes of Ballysumaghan and Kilross: the chapel is a thatched building in very indifferent repair, situated at Sooey. Two schools, in which about 50 boys and 30 girls are taught, are supported by private subscriptions. At Carrickcoola there are some inconsiderable remains of an old castle. On the lands of Ballinakill is a holy well, dedicated the Blessed Virgin to which the peasantry resort on Sept. 8th to perform certain devotions; and near it is a large rock, in which there are several natural caverns of very small dimensions.

BALLINTOGHER, a village, in the parish of Killery, barony of Tirerill 3 miles (S.W.) from Dromahair; containing 201 inhabitants. This place, which is situated on the road from Dromahair to Collooney, comprises about 40 thatched dwellings, and contains the parish church, a small plain building, and the parochial Roman Catholic chapel, a large and commodious edifice. Fairs are held on Jan. 22nd, June 8th, July 28th, Oct 17th, and Dec 8th; and here is a station of the constabulary police. Near it is Oldcastle, the residence of E. Loftus Neynoe, Esq; occupying the site of the ancient castle of Kingsfort. Iron ore has been found in the vicinity; and in the mountains west of Lough Gill are indications of coal, manganese, iron, and copper, besides a great variety of clays.-See KILLERY.

BALLYMOTE, a market and post-town, in the parish of Emlaghfad, barony of Corran, 11 miles (S. by W.) from Sligo, and 94 miles (W.N.W.) from Dublin; containing 875 inhabitants. This place appears to have derived its origin from a castle built in 1300 by Richard de Burgo, Earl of Ulster, which, after its seizure by the native Irish during the insurrection of 1641, was found to be of such strength as to offer a serious obstacle to the complete subjugation of Connaught; it was at length taken, in 1652, by the united forces of Ireton and Sir C. Coote. A small monastery for Franciscan friars of the third order was founded here by the sept of Mac Donogh, and at the suppression was granted to Sir H. Broncard, who assigned it to Sir W.Taaffe, Knt.: an inquisition of the 27th of Elizabeth records that it belonged to the castle and had been totally destroyed by the insurgents. The town is situated at the junction of six roads, but has not one principal road passing through it: it consists of one main street, and contains 140 houses. The surrounding country is well cultivated, and its surface agreeably undulates; and there is a good view from an obelisk erected by Lady Arabella Denny on a small hill near the town. In the immediate vicinity is Earlsfield the property of Sir Gore-Booth, Bart., to whom the town belongs; and in a delightful situation, within a quarter of a mile, is the glebe-house, which commands a fine prospect of the surrounding mountains and the distant hill of Knocknarea. About 2 miles from the town is Templehouse, the handsome residence of Col. A. Perceval, beautifully situated on the banks of a lake of that name, and in a fine demesne containing some good old timber; on the edge of the lake are the ruins of the old house, which was built by the O'Hara family in 1303, and was afterwards given to the Knights Hospitallers. The linen manufacture was formerly carried on here to a great extent, under the encouragement of the Rt. Hon. Thos. Fitzmaurice, but is now nearly extinct. The market is held on a Friday for provisions; and fairs are held on the last Monday in January, May 11th, first Monday (O.S.) in June, Sept.3rd, first Monday (O.S.) in November, and second Monday (O.S.) in December. Quarter sessions are held here in a sessions-house in

January, April, July, and October; and petty sessions on the alternate Tuesdays. The bridewell is the only one in the county: it affords the requisite statutable accommodation, and there are a day-room and airing-yard for prisoners of each sex. This is a chief station of the constabulary police. The parish church is situated in the town; and there is a R.C. chapel, a meeting-house for Wesleyan Methodists and a dispensary. The remains of the ancient castle, built by Richard de Burgo, occupy an area 150 feet square, with towers at the angles, and sufficiently denote its former strength. At the southern extremity of the main street are the ruins of the Franciscan friary; over the principal entrance is the figure of a pope carved in stone but somewhat mutilated. A book, called the Book or Psalter of Ballymote, was written in Irish by the monks of this place, and is yet extant. There is a fort of rather unusual elevation about one mile from the town. – See EMLAGHFAD.

BALLYSADARE,

or BALLISODARE, a parish, partly in the barony of Leyney but chiefly in that of Tirerill, comprising the post-town of Collooney, and the villages of Ballydrehid and Tubberscanavan (all of which are separately described); and containing 7,562 inhabitants, of which number, 546 are in the village. It is situated on the road from Boyle to Sligo, and on the Unchin or Ballysadare river, which, after falling over several ledges of rocks, the last of which is ten feet in height, empties itself into an arm of the sea, called Ballysadare channel. St. Fechin founded a monastery here towards the middle of the seventh century, which was richly endowed: in 1179 it was burnt, and in 1188 was again destroyed by fire, but was restored and existed until the general dissolution, when a lease of it was granted, in the 30th of Eliz., for 21 years, to Bryan Fitz-William, at an annual rent of £2.13.4.: the remains are situated above the waterfalls, and consist merely of the outer walls, which are richly clothed with ivy. St Fechin also founded an abbey at Killnamanagh which existed till the general suppression, when it was granted to Richard, Earl of Clanricarde; there are yet some remains. The parish comprises 9,999 statute acres, as applotted under the tithe act: between one third and one-half of it is waste land and bog; there is little woodland, except for 600 to 700 acres on the Markree estate.

The ruined Franciscan Friary, Ballymote, known locally as 'The Abbey'.

Ballymote Castle, built in the year 1300 by Richard de Burgh, the second Earl of Ulster, who was commonly called 'The Red Earl'.

The land under cultivation is generally good, but the old system of tillage, though gradually improving, is still mostly practised. There are quarries of excellent limestone, much used for building, and some of it is also hewn into mantel-pieces and other ornamental parts of masonry; and a lead mine, yielding a considerable proportion of silver, was worked a few years since, but has been abandoned. Near it are some chalybeate springs, not used. The village of Ballysadare, which comprised about 45 houses, is a place of little business, and has a penny post. The falls on the river afford favourable sites, and a never-failing supply of water for mills: there is a large corn-mill, belonging to Mr. Sim, worked by two wheels of 36-horse power, and employing 25 persons, and another on a large scale, with the most improved machinery, built by Mr. Culbertson in 1835, having two water-wheels of 70-horse power, and employing 20 persons; there are also some smaller corn-mills and a large bleach-mill and green. Vessels of about 100 tons' burden come up the channel for the exportation of corn and meal: a small pier has been built and it is in contemplation to erect one on a more extensive scale. Fairs are held at the village on Feb. 8th, May 30th, July 11th, Aug. 4th, Oct. 24th, Nov. 12th, and Dec. 15th; and besides those held at Collooney and Tubberscanavan (which are enumerated in the accounts of those places), the largest fair for horses in the county is held at Carricknagat on Feb. 1st. Here is a station of the constabulary police. Petty sessions are held every alternate Thursday at Collooney; and a manorial court is occasionally held there, under the seneschal. Markree, the seat of E.J. Cooper, Esq; is a handsome and modern castellated building, situated in the centre of an extensive demesne clothed with wood and spreading into verdant lawns, through which the Unchin pursues a winding course: the gateways leading into the demesne are handsome structures, of ancient English architecture, and in the grounds there is a very excellent observatory. The other seats are Cloonamahon, that of J. Meredith, Esq; the Cottage, of R. Culbertson, jun., Esq, Ballysadare House, of J. Reed, Esq; and Ballysadare Villa, of A. Sim Esq; The living is a vicarage, in the diocese of Achonry, constituting the corps of the prebend of Ballysadare, in the patronage of the Bishop: the rectory is impropriate in Matthew

Baker, Esq.: the tithes amount to £461.10.0., payable in moieties to the impropriator and the incumbent. The church, situated at Collooney, is a handsome building, in the English style of architecture, and contains some good monuments, of which one to the memory of the late Mrs. Cooper, executed at Florence, is a fine piece of Sculpture: it was enlarged in 1834, by aid of a gift of £700 from the Ecclesiastical Commissioners, and donations of £800 from Mr. Cooper and £50 from Major O'Hara. The glebe-house was built by aid of a gift of £400 and a loan of £400, in 1819, from the late Board of First Fruits: the glebe comprises 20 acres. In the R.C. divisions this parish is the head of a union or district, called Collooney, comprising also the parish of Kilvarnet and containing three chapels, situated respectively at Collooney and Corhownagh, in Ballysadare, and the third in Kilvarnet. There are seven schools, two of which, at Ballysadare and Collooney, were built and are supported by Mr. Cooper; also five private pay schools and Sunday schools. On an eminence immediately over the harbour is an ancient burial-ground of considerable extent, still used, in which are the remains of a church.

BALLYSUMAGHAN, a parish in the barony of Tirerill, 4 miles (E. by S.) from Collooney; containing 1,815 inhabitants. This parish is situated on the road from Sligo to Drumsna, by way of Ballyfarnon, on the confines of the count; and comprises 2,829 statute acres, as applotted under the tithe act. The soil is principally a good deep loam, but the state of agriculture, though much improved within the last twenty years, is still very low; there is not much waste land, but a very large tract of bog affording a good supply of fuel. There are several quarries of stone, principally limestone of a very fine description, used for building and for burning into lime. The gentlemen's seats are Castle Neynoe, that of Col. W.B. Neynoe, and Doonally of Owen Phibbs, Esq; The French Army, after the battle of Collooney, passed close to this place, and encamped the same night within a quarter of a mile from it. It is a vicarage, in the diocese of Elphin, and forms part of the union of Boyle; the rectory is partly impropriate to Viscount Lorton, and partly appropriate to the prebend of Kilmacallan in the cathedral church of Elphin. The tithes amount to £73.16.11., of which one-half is payable to the prebendary. The church is a neat building, erected about six years since on a site in the demesne of Castle Neynoe, given by Col. Neynoe; and the Ecclesiastical Commissioners have lately granted £181 for its repair: it is resorted to by the inhabitants of Ballysumaghan, Kilross, and Ballinakill, three of the parishes which form the union. Near to it is the glebe, but there is no glebe-house at present. In the R.C. division it is included in the union or district of Sooey. There is a school in the village of Castle Neynoe, and another at Bloomfield, in which about 100 boys and 90 girls are taught. A Sunday school is held in the church, and it is in contemplation to establish a parochial school: there is also a hedge school, in which are about 40 boys and 30 girls. Within the parish are several Danish forts; and in the burial-ground of Kiltycloghan are the remains of an old church. Numerous fossils are found in the limestone quarries.

BANADA, a village in the parish of Kilmacteigue, 3 miles (W. by S.) from Tubbercurry: the population is returned with the parish. It comprises about 30 cabins and is beautifully situated on the banks of the river Moy, which winds through it in a broad deep stream, and on the road from Tubbercurry to Foxford. A friary of Eremites, following the rule of St. Augustine, was founded here in 1423, through the industry of a brother of that order, and was dedicated to Corpus Christi. The modern seat, called the Abbey, is the residence of D. Jones, Esq., and from a plantation rises the lofty steeple of the ancient monastery, built of hewn stone and still entire. Fairs are held on Jan. 17th, May 19th, and Aug. 7th; and here is a station of the constabulary police. See KILMACTEIGUE

BELLAGHY, a village, in the parish of Achonry, 10 miles (S.W.) from Ballymote, on the road to Swinford; containing 34 houses and 170 inhabitants. A market for provisions is held on Wednesday, and a fair is held every month: the market-house is situated in the centre of the village. Here is a station of the constabulary police. – See ACHONRY.

CALRY, a parish, in the barony of Carbury; containing, with a part of the borough and sea-port town of Sligo, 6,247 inhabitants, of which number 3,741 are within the Borough of Sligo. This parish is situated on the river Garavogue, which separates it from the parish

Hazlewood

Hazlewood House, an early 18th century Palladian style residence built of cut stone and polished limestone in the Italian style to style to the design of Richard Cassells. For over two centuries it was the seat of the influental Wynne family, who were burgesses of Sligo Corporation and members of Parliament for both town and county.

of St. John, it its course from Lough Gill to the sea, and on the roads from Ballyshannon and Enniskillen to Sligo. It contains 4,383 statute acres, as applotted under the tithe act: the land is generally light, with a small quantity of bog and some mountain wastes, and is principally under tillage; the state of agriculture is improving; there is an abundance of limestone, which is used for building. The manufacture of linen was formerly carried on extensively, but few are now employed in it. Lough Gill, part of which is in the parish, is an extensive and beautiful sheet of water, about a mile and a half from Sligo, with which it is connected by the river Garavogue, that is navigable for large boats seven or eight miles. The scenery is very romantic, and is greatly embellished with the highly cultivated demesne of Hazelwood, the handsome residence of Owen Wynne, Esq; The Lough is studded with islands, of which Church and Cottage islands are the largest. At Hollywell is another demesne belonging to Mr. Wynne, from which mountains covered with wood, the lake with its numerous islands, and the road sometimes running under stupendous rocks and sometimes through small

planted glens, present scenes of great beauty. The other seats are Percymount, that of Sir Percy Gethin, Bart; Colga House, of T. Homan, Esq.; Willsboro', of W. Fausset, Esq.; Willowbrook, of the Ormsby family; Barroe House, of Follis Clarke, Esq.; Rathbraughan Cottage, of W. Christian, Esq.; Mount Shannon, of H.H. Slade, Esq.; Shannon, of Edward Patterson, Esq.; the Cottage, of J. Gethin, Esq.; Ballytivnan House, of Mrs. Griffith, and Ellenville, of H. Irwin, Esq.; M.D.

The living consists of a vicarage and perpetual curacy, in the diocese of Elphin, the former being part of the union of St. John's Sligo, and the latter in the patronage of the Incumbent of St. John's; the rectory is appropriate to the vicars choral of the cathedral of Christ-Church, Dublin. The tithes amount to £353.11.7., payable in moieties to the vicars choral and the vicar. The income of the perpetual curacy amounts to £73.1.6., arising from £23.1.6. paid by the Ecclesiastical Commissioners, and £50 from the vicars choral. The church, belonging to the perpetual cure, is a handsome structure in the later English style, with a beautiful spire: it was built by aid of a gift and loan from the late Board of

Calry Church, The Mall, built in 1823 in the Gothic style as a 'chapel of ease' for St. John's Church, overlooks the river Garvogue. It's graceful spire is a well known landmark.

First Fruits, in 1823. The glebe-house was also built by aid of a gift of £112 and a loan of £37, in 1821, from the same Board. In the R.C. divisions this parish forms part of the union or district of Sligo; the chapel is at Colga. Here are a school established and supported by the trustees of Erasmus Smith's charity; a female parochial school at Calry; and a school at Ballinorley, which was built by John Wynne, Esq., at an expense of £250, and supported by that gentleman. About 120 boys and 70 girls are educated in these schools; and there are also a private school of 50 boys and 30 girls, and five Sunday schools. The part of the parish that is within the Town of Sligo contains the County Infirmary, Fever Hospital, and Dispensary. The remains of antiquity consist of the Sod Fort, which was defended by Sir Teague O'Regan against the forces of King William, the ruins of some churches in Church and Cottage islands, and what are supposed to be druidical remains in Mr. Wynne's part at Hazelwood.

CARNEY, a village, in the parish of Drumcliffe, 5 miles (N.W.) from Sligo; containing 45 houses and 220 inhabitants. It is situated on the bay of Drumcliffe, about a half a mile to the left of the road from Sligo to Ballyshannon; and has a market on Thursday and fairs on May 26th and June 24th, chiefly for cattle and sheep. A constabulary police force is stationed here; and dispensary is supported principally by Sir R. Gore-Booth, Bart.
See DRUMCLIFFE

CASTLECONNOR, a parish, in the barony of Tireragh, 4 miles (N. and E.) from Ballina; containing 4,507 inhabitants. This place derives its name from an ancient castle, of which the ruins are still visible; and is situated on the river Moy and on the road from Ballina to Sligo. The parish comprises 16,223 statute acres, as applotted under the tithe act; the greater portion is under an improving system of tillage, and there are some large stock farms; there is a considerable extent of bog, and abundance of limestone is quarried for agricultural and other purposes. The principal seats are Moyview, that of the Hon. Col. Wingfield; Cottlestown, of S. Kirkwood, Esq.; Knockroe House, of G. Ruttledge, Esq.; Seaville, of P.I. Howley, Esq.; and Kinnard, of J. Paget, Esq;. The living is a vicarage, in the diocese of Killala, united by act of Council, in 1806 to the vicarage of Kilglass;

the rectory, formerly appropriate to the See, is now sequestrated in the Ecclesiastical Commissioners. The tithes amount to £4776.6.1., one-half of which is payable to the Ecclesiastical Commissioners, and the other to the vicar. The church was built by aid of a gift of £900 from the late Board of First Fruits, in 1818. The glebe-house was built in 1820, by aid of a gift of £100 and a loan of £675 from the same Board: the glebe of the union comprises 50 acres. The R.C. parish is co-extensive with that of the Established Church; the chapel is at Castletown. A school is supported at Dooneen; and there are three pay schools, in which are 240 children. Here is also a dispensary. There are some remains of the old castle on the bank of the Moy, and of the old church of Killanly with a burial ground. There are also some Danish raths.

CHURCH ISLAND
or INNISMORE ISLAND, in

the parish of Calry, 3 miles (E.) from Sligo; containing, in 1821, 9 inhabitants. It is situated in Lough Gill, and contains 180 acres, the property of Owen Wynne, Esq. St. Loman founded a church here in the time of St. Columb, the ruins of which still exist at the east end of the island, overgrown with ivy. The abbey was accidentally destroyed by fire in 1416, in which the valuable manuscripts of O'Curnin, together with the short book of that family, and many other rare curiosities, perished. In former ages it was the burial-place of the parishioners.

CLOONOGHILL, a parish, in the barony of Corran, 3 miles (W.S.W.) from Ballymote, on the road from Boyle to Ballina; containing 2,241 inhabitants. This place was formerly called Cloonameehan and was the seat of a Dominican monastery, founded about 1488, by the sept of Mac Donogh, which afterwards became a cell to that of Sligo: at the dissolution its possessions were granted to Richard Kyndelinshe. The parish contains 4,551 statute acres, as applotted under the tithe act: the land is generally good, and there is not much bog. Limestone quarries are worked here. Fairs are held at Bunninadden on Jan. 14th, June 2nd, Aug. 6th, Sept. 10th, Oct. 7th, and Nov. 27th. The principal seats are Ballinaglogh, the residence of J. West, Esq.; Grayfort, of J. Rea, Esq.; Roadstown of D. O'Connor, Esq.; Drumrane, of J. Taaffe, Esq.; and

Old Rock, of J. Trumble, Esq.; It is a rectory and vicarage, in the diocese of Achonry; the rectory is partly impropriate to J. Baker, Esq.; and partly, with the vicarage, forms a portion of the union and corps of the deanery of Achonry. The tithes amount to £170 per annum, of which £90 is payable to the impropriator and the remainder to the dean. In the R. C. divisions it is the head of a union or district, called Bunninadden, comprising the parishes of Cloonoghill, Kilturra, and Kilshalvey; and containing two chapels, of which that of Cloonoghill, at Bunninadden, is a large slated building. There is a school at Ballinaglogh, under the patronage of J. West, Esq.; in which are about 100 children; and there is also a hedge school for 50 children. On the banks of the river are the remains of an old castle, built by the Mac Donoghs; and on the lands of Church Hill is a large cromlech, consisting of a horizontal and three upright stones.

COLLOONEY, a post-town, in that part of the parish of Ballysadare which is in the barony of Tirerill, 5 miles (S.) from Sligo, on the road to Dublin, and 98 (N.W.) from Dublin containing 553 inhabitants. It consists of one long street; containing 90 houses, of which 13 are slated, and the remainder thatched. At Carricknagat the French, after quitting Castlebar, were attacked on 5th Sept., 1798, by Col. Vereker, with a detachment of the city of Limerick militia, some yeomanry, and the 24th light dragoons; but after a smart action of about an hour and a half, the colonel was nearly surrounded, and obliged to retreat, with the loss of his artillery, to Sligo, whence he withdrew to Ballyshannon. The assault was sufficient, as it is supposed, to deter the French from attacking Sligo, and they marched to Dromahaire. The market is on Thursday; and the fairs were formerly held on May 3rd, June 1st, Aug. 9th, Sept. 5th, Nov. 21st, and Dec. 16th, but that of Nov. 21st is the only one now held. Here are a large bleaching establishment and an oatmeal-mill. Near the town are Annaghmore, the residence of C. K. O'Hara, Esq.; and Camphill, of A. Kelly, Esq;. In the town are the parish church and a R. C.chapel, a linen-hall, a dispensary and two schools. It is a station of the constabulary policy. (See BALLYSADARE)

CONEY ISLAND, an island, in the parish of Killaspugbrone, the population is returned with the

Longford House, Beltra, a large late 18th century residence, built of rough cut ashlar, seat of the Crofton family until badly damaged by an accidental fire and never fully restored.

parish. This island, which is situated in the bay of Sligo, was anciently called *Inishmulcloghy,* and is enumerated among the territories settled on the Earl of Strafford and Sir Thomas Radcliffe, in 1663. It is at present the property of J. Meredith, Esq., and near it are the ruins of the ancient parish church of Killaspugbrone, nearly covered with sand.

COOLANEY, a small market town, in the parish of Killoran, 4 miles (W.) from Collooney; containing 326 inhabitants. This place is situated on the road from Sligo to Tubbercurry; it contains about 70 houses, and has a penny post to Collooney. Here are a dispensary and a Baptist meeting-house; and it is a station of the constabulary police. In the centre of the village is the court-house, where petty sessions are held on alternate Wednesdays. The market is on Friday, and fairs are held on the 29th May and 15th December: it is in contemplation to erect a market-house. – See KILLORAN

CURRY, a village in the parish of Achonry, 9 miles (S.W.) from Ballymote, on the road to Swinford, containing about 40 houses and 167 inhabitants. It

gives its name to the R.C. district, the parochial chapel of which stands here. Fairs are held on Ascension day, Corpus Christi, and Aug.9th.

DERNISH, or DERRINISH, an island, in the parish to Ahamlish, 10 miles (N.N.E.) from Sligo: the population is returned with the parish. This island is situated near the entrance of Milkhaven, on the north-west, and contains about 76 statute acres of land, the property of Lord Palmerston. On its south-west side is safe anchorage in all weather in two fathoms. Milkhaven is situated about three leagues east of the point of Ballyconnell; the entrance is difficult, and only adapted for vessels drawing from 6 to 8 feet of water.

DROMARD, a parish, in the barony of Tireragh, 5 miles (W.) from Collooney, on the road from Sligo to Ballina; containing 2,560 inhabitants. The Cromwellians captured this place and burnt the old bawn of Tanrego. In the reign of Wm. 111., the castle of Longford successfully resisted two attacks of a detachment of the troops under Major Vaughan; numerous skeletons of men and horses are constantly being dug up

Markree Castle, the ancestral seat of the Cooper family, was originally surrounded by a large demense, one of the finest in County Sligo. It now functions as a hotel.

in the demesne, where the battle was fought. The parish comprises 4,923 statute acres, as applotted under the tithe act, and there is a considerable tract of unreclaimed mountain land. Here are quarries of limestone and granite of the best description. Fairs are held at Beltra on the Monday before Ash Wednesday, May 21st, and August 20th. The principal seats are Tanrego, the residence of Col. Irwin, a very old mansion which commands remarkably fine views of the bays of Sligo, Donegal and Killybegs; the glebe-house was built in 1833, by aid of a gift of £350 and a loan of £450 from the late Board of First Fruits: the glebe comprises 15 acres. The church, a neat plain building with a square tower, was erected by the grandfather of Col. Irwin, and subsequently enlarged in 1818, by aid of a loan of £600 from the same board. The R.C. parish is co-extensive with that Established Church, and has a good slated chapel at Altanelvick. Here is a school of about 40 boys and 40 girls, under the trustees of Erasmus Smith's charity; the school-house is a stone slated building, erected at an expense of about £250 on an acre of land given by Col. Irwin. The Rev. Dr. Benton, late rector of the parish, left £299 late currency, which is now vested in the Commissioners of Charitable bequests, and the interest distributed among the poor at Easter. Near the river of Ballinlig are the ruins of an old religious house; and there are some remains of the old church, near which is a holy well, dedicated to St. Patrick. In the demesne of Longford is an old R.C. chapel, now disused; it was built by the O'Dowds, from whom the Croftons inherit the estate.

DROMORE-WEST, a village and post-town in the parish of Kilmacshalgan, 18 miles (W.S.W.) from Sligo, and 113 (N.N.W.) from Dublin, on the mail coach road from Sligo to Ballina; containing 109 inhabitants. It consists of about 20 houses, and in the vicinity are several gentlemen's residences, of which Dromore House is the seat of John Fenton, Esq. Fairs are held on the first Thursday in Jan., June 6th and Dec.29th. A revenue police force has been stationed here, and there is a R.C. chapel.

DRUMCLIFFE, a parish, in the barony of Carbury, 3 miles (N.N.W.)from Sligo, on the mail coach road to Londonderry, through Ballyshannon; containing 13,956 inhabitants. This place

The westside of the 'Great Cross' at Drumcliffe, generally regarded as a 'gem' amongst Irish antiquities.

49

anciently called Cnoc na teagh, was once a large town. A monastery was founded here, in 590, by St. Columba, who appointed his disciple, St. Thorian, or Mothorian, abbot, and to his office Episcopal jurisdiction was united: the See was subsequently united to Elphin. St. Torannan, a succeeding abbot, who died in 921, was afterwards regarded as the patron saint of the place. The parish comprises 17,038 statute acres, as applotted under tillage, and there is abundance of bog. On the north-west side of Maugherow lies the Serpent Rock, so called from the great variety of its curious fossils, representing serpents, and fishes. Here are quarries of limestone; and at Glencar is a remarkable waterfall, 300 feet high; but when the wind is south, the water is prevented from descending. At Raughley is a good harbour, designed by Mr. Mimmo, and executed at the joint expense of the Government and Sir R. Gore-Booth, Bart. Petty sessions are held at Summerhill every Wednesday; and a major court is held at Ardtarmon under Sir R. Gore-Booth's patent. The principal seats are Lissadell, the residence of Sir R. Gore-Booth, Bart; Cregg House of the Hon. R. King; Dunally, of Col. Parke; Ellen-villa,

of J. C. Martin, Esq.; Summerhill, of . Irwin, Esq.; Elsinore of R. Young, Esq.; Mount Shannon, of H.H. Slade, Esq., Cottage of J. Gethin, Esq., Willowbrook, of W. Ormsby-Gore, Esq., and Millbrook, of J. Simpson, Esq. The living is a vicarage, in the diocese of Elphin, and in the patronage of the Bishop; the rectory is impropriate in Owen Wynne, Esq. The tithes amount to £720 of which half is paid to the impropriator and half to the vicar. The glebe-house stands on a glebe of 40 acres. The church is a handsome building in the Gothic style, with a square town ornamented with minarets, erected by aid of a loan of £800, in 1809, from the late Board of First Fruits, on part of the site of the ancient abbey: the church service is also performed every Sunday in the school-house at Lissadell. In the R.C. divisions this parish is divided into two parts, Drumcliffe and Rathcormac: and has three chapels. There is a place of worship for Wesleyan Methodists at Drum, and one for Primitive Methodists. Schools at Milltown and Castletown are supported by Sir R. Gore-Booth, Bart.; at Drum, by J. Wynne, Esq.; and there are two other public schools. In these about 500 children are educated, and in twelve private schools about

The Old Bridge of Drumcliffe as depicted on an 19th Century Estate Map

700 are taught; there are also four Sunday schools. There are some remains of the monastic buildings, and close to the shore are the ruins of the ancient castle of the Gore family, which settled here in the reign of Wm.111.; there is also a portion of an ancient round tower; and near the church are two remarkable crosses, one handsomely carved, the other mutilated. In the demesne of Summerhill is an extensive Danish fort, called Lisnalurg and, near Lissadell demesne, a cromlech weighing several tons. There are also many ancient forts, one having a chamber underground; and at Raughley are chalybeate springs. - See CARNEY.

DRUMCOLLUMB, a parish, in the barony of Tirerill, 10 miles (N. by W.) from Boyle, on the road to Sligo; containing 1,652 inhabitants. It comprises 2,807 statute acres, as applotted under the tithe act: the soil is generally good, but there is much marsh and bog. Here is Lisconny, the residence of B. O. Cogan, Esq. It is a vicarage, in the diocese of Elphin, forming part of the union of Boyle; the rectory is appropriate to the prebend of Kilmacallan in Elphin cathedral. The tithes amount to £83.1.6., which are paid to the incumbent of Boyle, who is also prebendary of Kilmacallan. In the R.C. divisions it forms part of the union or district of Riverstown. About 50 children are educated in a public school. There is a burial-place, in which are the ruins of a church, said to have been founded by St. Columb.

DRUMRAT, a parish, in the barony of Corran, 3 miles (S.) from Ballymote, on the road from Boyle to Ballymote; containing 1,606 inhabitants. It is on the confines of the county of Roscommon, and comprises 3,682 statute acres, as applotted under the tithe act. The land is principally under tillage, and there is a due portion of good grazing land, with a sufficient tract of bog for fuel. Limestone is quarried for agricultural purposes. Abbeyville is the residence of J. Fleming, Esq. It is in the diocese of Achonry; the rectory is impropriate to Sir H. Montgomery, Bart., and the vicarage forms part of the union of Emlaghfad. The tithes amount to £204.13.11., of which £95.3.3 is payable to the impropriator, and £109.10.8. to the vicar. In the R.C. divisions the parish forms part of the union or district of Toomour; the chapel is in Culfadda. There are two private schools, in which are about 90 boys and 40 girls. An abbey was founded here by St. Fechin, of which the last abbot of whom there is any record, died in 1016; it afterwards became the parish church, and there are still some remains.

EASKEY, a parish, in the barony of Tireragh, 11 miles (N.N.E.) from Ballina, on the road to Sligo; containing 6,124 inhabitants, of which number, 289 are in the village. The parish is situated on the north-west coast, between the entrances to the bays of Sligo and Killala; it includes the Point of Kinesharrow, called also Rathlee Point, and comprises 12,977 statute acres, principally under an improving system of tillage; there is a large quantity of bog. Limestone, which abounds with fossils, is found on the sea shore; much sea-weed is collected for manure. The village consists of one long street of 76 houses, and has petty sessions once a fortnight, a market on Wednesday for provisions, fairs on June 3rd and Nov. 18th, and is a chief constabulary police station; fairs are also held at Rosslee in July, and on Oct. 28th. Fortland, pleasantly situated on the banks of the river Easkey, is the residence of R. Jones Esq., proprietor of the salmon fishery here; Castletown, of T. Fenton, Esq.; and Rathlee, of T. Jones, Esq. The living is a vicarage, in the diocese of Killala, and in the patronage of the Bishop: the rectory is appropriate to the See. The tithes amount to £586.14.5., equally divided between the bishop and the vicar. The glebe-house, on a glebe of nine acres, was build by a gift of £300, and a loan of £500 from the late Board of First Fruits, in 1815. The church is a neat building with a square tower, erected by aid of a loan of £1,342, from the same Board; the Ecclesiastical Commissioners have recently granted £130 for its repair. The R.C. parish is co-extensive with that of the Established Church, and contains a chapel. Here is also a place of worship for Baptists. About 600 children are educated in five public schools; and at Killenduff is a school supported by Col. Irwin, who built the school house, and endowed it with three acres of land. In the village are the ruins of the old parish church; and there are considerable remains of the old castle of Rosslee, formerly belonging to the O'Dowds, and, on the opposite side of the river, the remains of another, on the lands of Castletown. There are several Danish forts, and on the lands of

Napoleonic 'Look Out' Tower: at Carrowmably, Dromore West

Roslea Castle, Easkey, as depicted in Francis Grose's *Antiquities of Ireland 1797*.
It was originally a stronghold of the O'Dowds.

Tawnamaddoo is a cromlech, seven feet high, and supported by four square pillars. The shores of the parish are bold and rocky, and abound with curiosities. At Alternan is a station, holy well, and saints bed, named after St. Farannan, and much frequented by pilgrims; the patron is held on the last Sunday in July. Near Fortland is a chalybeate spring.

EMLAGHFAD, a parish, in the barony of Corran, containing, with the post town of Ballymote (which is described under its own head), 4,645 inhabitants; and comprising 9,915 statute acres, chiefly pasture, with some bog. Agriculture is improving; there are quarries of good limestone in the parish. The gentlemen's seats are Carrowkeel, that of F. MacDonagh, Esq.; Drumrane, of J. Taaffe, Esq., Templehouse, of Col. A. Perceval; the glebe-house, of the Rev. J. Garrett; and Earlsfield, the property of Sir R. Gore-Booth, Bart. The living is a vicarage, in the diocese of Achonry, united by act of council, in 1807, to Kilmorgan, Kilturra, Toomour, and Drumrat, together forming the union of Emlaghfad, in the patronage of the Bishop; the rectory is impropriate partly in Sir H.C. Montgomery, Bart., and partly in the Earl of Kingston. The tithes amount to £407. 7. 7, of which £168. 1.6, is payable to Sir H. Montgomery, and £239.6 1, to the vicar, from the latter sum the Earl of Kingston claims £40; and the gross amount of the tithes of the benefice is £170. The glebe house was built by aid of a gift of £100 and a loan of £600, in 1810, from the late Board of First Fruits; the glebe comprises 20 acres. The church, at Ballymote, is a good building in the early English style, remarkable for the beauty of its tower and spire ; it was erected by aid of loans of £550, in 1818, and £1000, in 1831, from the late Board, and donations of £300 from the Earl of Orkney, and £100 each from the Bishop of Killala and E.S. Cooper, Esq. The Ecclesiastical Commissioners have recently granted £190 for its repair. In the R.C. divisions this is the head of a union or district, also called Ballymote, comprising this parish and that of Kilmorgan, in each of which is a chapel; that in Ballymote is a large building. There is also a place of worship for Wesleyan Methodists. In the parish are four public schools, of which the parochial school is aided by Sir R. Gore Booth, Viscount Lorton, and local subscriptions, and in which are about 100 children. The ruins of the old church , with its steeple, form a conspicuous object, from their elevated situation. An abbey is said to have been founded here by St, Columb, over which his disciple St Enna presided. On the edge of Templehouse lake are the ruins of an old house, once inhabited by the Knights Templars; and near Ballymote is a fort of considerable elevation.

GRANGE, a village in the parish of Ahamlish, 8 miles (N.) from Sligo, on the road to Ballyshannon; containing 221 inhabitants. It comprises 40 houses, and has two bridges which were erected at the close of the last century. It is a revenue and constabulary police station, and has fairs, on June 2nd and 28th , July 25th, August 25th, Sept 29th, Oct 28th, and Dec 10th.

INISHMURRAY, an island in the parish of Ahamlish, 15 miles (N) from Sligo; containing 87 inhabitants . This island is situated in the Atlantic Ocean, about five miles off the western coast, and 2 leagues (N.N.E.) from Ballyconnell point. A religious establishment was founded on it by St Columb, in conjunction with St Molaise, to whom he relinquished the whole government, and who consequently became the patron

saint of the island. This little monastery, which was dedicated to the Blessed Virgin, was destroyed by the Danes in 804. In 1666, the island with all its appurtenances was granted by Chas. 11. to the Earl of Strafford and Thomas Radcliffe, Esq., and is now the property of Viscount Palmerston. It consists of a vast rock rising precipitously towards the ocean and shelving gradually towards the mainland, and comprises about 126 acres of profitable land, chiefly affording pasturage to a few horses, cows, and sheep, with a large tract of turbary, which, though shallow supplies a good hard turf impregnated with a large portion of bituminous matter. The soil of that portion which is under tillage is light, and though every means have been used to enrich the land with sea manure, the results in general are unfavourable. The inhabitants, consisting of about 18 families, and occupying about the same number of dwellings, form a community, generally intermarrying with each other, and speaking their original language. They are chiefly employed in fishing, and during the winter, when the island is inaccessible, in making whiskey. The sea affords abundance of fish, including pollock, mackerel, lobsters, crabs,

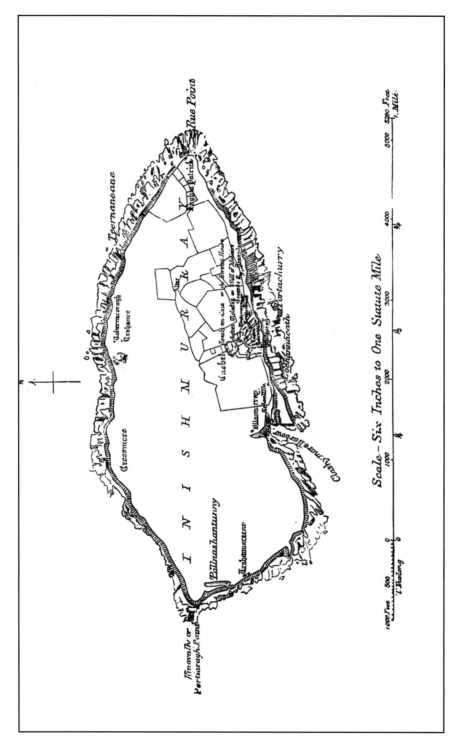

The Island of Inishmurray, which can boast of the most complete and visually exciting early Christian and monastic settlement in Europe.

and other shellfish, which form their chief subsistence and are their articles of trade with the mainland. There is an abundant supply of fresh water; and on the north side of the island is a quarry of good granite. There are some remains of the old religious buildings, which were of the rudest construction. In one, resembling a fort and built of rude stones, is a figure of St Molaise carved in oak, about 3 feet high: the east end of this chapel, which is not more than 7 feet long and 4 feet wide, is covered with very fine flags , and the whole surrounded with a wall enclosing about half an acre. There are several compartments excavated in the rock , which appear to have been cells for solitary prayer; one of these is covered with a flag of the size and form of a millstone ; and near it is a large flag stone , supported on 8 upright stones about two feet high, on which are placed about 40 or 50 stones called by the people Clocha-Breacha or "the cursing stones" from a belief that by turning them , and at the same time invoking imprecations against those by whom they suspect to have been injured , a curse will fall upon that person if guilty, but if innocent , on themselves. Of another stone it is said , that if the fire of the island be by neglect or accident extinguished, if fuel be laid on it, it will immediately be ignited. The cemeteries connected with the monastic ruins are appropriated to males and females respectively. On the east, west, and north points of the island are three buildings, supposed to have been the cells of anchor; and there is also a subterraneous cavern. About one mile to the north of the island is a rock, called Bomore, rising from a depth of eighty fathoms, the top of which at high water forms an area about five yards square , round which abundance of fish is caught and a submarine vegetable found in large quantities. The passage between the mainland and the island, called Inishmurray sound, is very dangerous to vessels making the passage to windward, with the wind from the west; for there are reefs extending from the mainland to the southward, where even in moderate weather is a heavy short sea. Two miles north of the island is the Boahinsky rock, always above water, at about a cables length from the east side of which is a rocky ledge, and about a quarter of a mile to the west a dry rock. A school is supported by Owen Wynne, Esq; lessee of the estate, who allows the master £10 per annum.

KILCOLMAN, a parish, partly in the barony of Coolavin, but chiefly in that of Costello, county of Mayo, on the new mail coach road from Longford to Ballina; containing, with the market and post-town of Ballaghadereen, 5,021 inhabitants. It comprises 13,030 statute acres, of which 5,880 are bog; and land is in general of very inferior quality, and the system of agriculture unimproved. Limestone is very scarce, but there are some quarries of freestone of very good quality. The seats are Edmondstown, the residence of the Costello family; Clogher, of R. Holmes, Esq.; and Coolavin House, of C.J. McDermot, Esq. The parish is in the diocese of Achonry; the rectory is impropriate to Lord Dillon, and the vicarage forms part of the union of Castlemore. There are six public schools, some of which are aided by donations from Lord Dillon, Mr. Holmes, and the incumbent, affording instruction to about 580 children; and there is a private school, in which are about 80 children. There are some remains of the old parish church.

KILFREE, a parish in the half-barony of Coolavin, 6 miles (W.) from Boyle, on the road from this place to Ballina; containing 5,103 inhabitants. The soil is good, the land principally in tillage, and there is abundance of turf and limestone. It is a constabulary police station, and a manorial court is held occasionally. The principal seats are Kilfree, the residence of E. Costello, Esq.: Mount Irwin, of W. T. Sherlock, Esq.; and Redhill, of A. Baker, Esq. It is a vicarage, in the diocese of Achonry, forming part of the union of Killaraght; the rectory is impropriate to Viscount Lorton, and the tithes amount to £287.0.8., which is equally divided between the impropriator and the vicar. The church is a plain building with a square tower, erected in 1826, for which the late Board of First Fruits granted a loan of £600. In the R. C. divisions it is the head of a union or district, called Gurteen, which comprises this parish and Killaraght, and has a large chapel in Gurteen, built in 1829, and one in Killaraght. About 59 children are educated in a public, and 260 in eight private, schools. A friary was erected at Knockmore in the 14th century, by O'Gara, of which the doorway and windows are in good preservation, and it is still a favourite burial-place. Here are also the ruins of O'Gara's Castle, the residence of that O'Gara who had the Psalter of Ballymote written, and whose descendant, Colonel O'Gara, left Ireland after the battle of Aughrim having forfeited his possessions, and entered the Austrian service.

KILGLASS, a parish in the barony of Tireragh, 8 miles (N.N.E.) from Ballina, on the bay of Killala; containing 4,275 inhabitants. Many of the peasantry who assembled here in 1798 were killed in an attack made by the cavalry. The parish comprises 12,478 statute acres, chiefly under tillage, with a considerable quantity of bog. Carrownedin is the property of E. Tennant, Esq., and Kinnard, is the residence of J. Paget, Esq. It is a vicarage, in the diocese of Killala, forming part of the union of Castleconnor; the rectory is appropriate to the bishopric, the deanery, and the precentorship of Killala. The tithes amount to £476, of which £234 is payable to the bishop, £4 to the dean, £4 to the precentor, and £234 to the vicar. The church is a neat building with a spire, erected in 1829 by aid of a gift of £900 from the late Board of First Fruits. There is a glebe of 17 acres, but no glebe-house. The R. C. parish is co-extensive with that of the Established Church, and contains a chapel, which was built in 1825, at an expense of £600. About 240 children are educated in three public schools, one of which is endowed with a bequest of £400 from the late Rev. J. Valentine, which has accumulated to £865: the school-house is a good stone building, and cost £215. About 370 children are educated in six private schools. At Enniscrone, in this parish, is a coast-guard station belonging to the Sligo district; also a constabulary police station. Petty sessions are held there on alternate Saturdays; and fairs are held on June 15th and Sept. 28th; one is also held at Quigaboy on July 20th. At Pullocheny creek, on the east side of the bay of Killala, small vessels land kelp, & c., in summer; it has tolerably good shelter in most winds behind the breakwater. The ruins of a castle are near this creek, and there are also ruins of castles at Enniscrone and Lacken.

KILLADOON, a parish in the barony of Tirerill, 7 miles (N.N.W.) from Boyle, on Lough Arrow; containing 1,525 inhabitants. The family of Mac Donogh, lords of Corran and Tirerill, founded a convent here, dedicated to the Blessed Virgin, for nuns of the order of St. Dominick in 1427; there are still some ruins on the northern shore of Lough Arrow. The parish comprises 6,364 statue acres as applotted under the tithe

Ballindoon Abbey, situated on the shores of Lough Arrow, was founded by the McDonaghs in 1427, in honour of the Virgin Mary for Dominican nuns. There were two chapels divided by a belfry. The eastern and western windows are Gothic and only part of the tower remains. It was the chief burial place of the McDonaghs of Tirerrill, including Terence McDonagh, the celebrated 18th Catholic Counsellor.

act, consisting principally of wet spongy land; there is a large quantity of bog, and limestone is quarried. It is a vicarage, in the diocese of Elphin, forming part of the union of Kilmactranny; the rectory is impropriated to Col. Perceval; the tithes amount to £42, which is equally divided between the impropriator and the vicar. In the R.C. divisions it is part of the union or district of Geevagh, or Kilmactranny. About 170 children are educated in two private schools.

KILLARAGHT, a parish in the half-barony of Coolavin, 4 miles (S. W.) from Boyle, on the road from that place to Frenchpark; containing 1,986 inhabitants. This place is said to derive its name from a nunnery founded here by St. Patrick for St. Attracta, who received the veil from him in 470. It is situated on the southern shore of Lough Gara, and consists chiefly of pasture land. The principal seats are Lisserlough, the residence of Jacob Powell, Esq.; Ardgallin, of Harlow P. Baker, Esq.; and Rathermon, of J. Flanagan, Esq. It is a vicarage, in the diocese of Achonry, episcopally united to those of Kilfree and Kilshalvey, the rectory is impropriate in Viscount Lorton. The tithes amount to £150,

of which £56. 9. 4. is payable to the impropriator, and £93.10.8. to the vicar. There is a glebe of 3 acres. In the R. C. divisions it forms part of the union or district of Gurteen, and has a chapel at Cloonloo. About 90 children are educated in a school that is aided by Lord Lorton. At Templeronan are the ruins of a church, with a burial-place attached.

KILLASPUGBRONE, a parish in the barony of Carbury 5 miles (W) from Sligo, on the bay of Sligo; containing with Coney and Oyster islands 1,812 inhabitants. It comprises 12,451 statute acres, as applotted under the tithe act. The land is principally in tillage, and there is some limestone, but no bog. It comprehends the glen of Knocknarea, which is about a mile in length and beautifully planted, with several cascades in the centre and stupendous rocks on each side; and at the western extremity is a fine view of the Ballysadare channel. At Culleenamore are some good beds of oysters. The principal seats are Culleenamore, the residence of S. Barrett, Esq.; Cummin, of T. Ormsby, Esq.; Glen Lodge, of M. Walsh, Esq.; Primrose Grange, of G.D. Meredith, Esq.; Rathcarrick, of J. Walker, Esq.; Strandhill, of G.

Meredith, Esq.; and Seafield, of Wm. Phibbs Esq. It is a rectory and vicarage, in the diocese of Elphin, forming part of the union of St. John's, Sligo: the tithes amount to £185. 1. 9. In the R.C. divisions it also forms part of the union or district of St. John's, Sligo, and has a good slated chapel at the base of Knocknarea Hill. At Primrose Grange there is a school for boarding, instructing, clothing, and apprenticing 110 boys, endowed by the late Edward Nicholson, Esq., of Sligo, with £130 per annum, and 20 acres of mountain land; about 25 children are educated in another public school. Here are the ruins of an ancient church said to have been founded by a bishop named Brone or, Bronus, from which the parish derives its name; but they are now nearly buried by the drifting sands, which have also covered about 400 acres of good land. There are numerous raths, especially near Rathcarrick.

KILLERY, a parish, in the barony of Tirerill, 4 miles (S.W.) from Dromahaire, on the road from that place to Collooney and on Lough Gill; containing 2,969 inhabitants. It comprises 9,135 statute acres, as applotted under the tithe act. The land is good quality, principally under tillage, and there is some bog and excellent limestone. Fairs are held at Ballintogher on Jan. 22nd, June 8th, July 28th, Oct. 17th and Dec. 8th; and a manorial court is held there occasionally. Oldcastle, the seat of E. Loftus Neynoe, Esq., was erected on the site of the old castle of Kingsfort; near it is a strong chalybeate spa. It is a vicarage, in the diocese of Ardagh, united to that of Killenumery; the rectory is impropriate in M. Baker, Esq. The tithes amount to £96. 18. 6., of which one-third is payable to the impropriator, and two-thirds to the vicar. The church is a plain building, erected in 1715. In the R. C. divisions it forms part of the union or district of Killenumery, and has a chapel at Ballintogher. About 140 children are educated in two public, and 1210 in two private schools. There are some remains of the old church of Killery, with a large burial-ground; and of an ancient castle at Drumcondra.

KILLORAN, a parish in the barony of Leyney, 6 miles (N.W.) from Ballymote, on the road from Sligo to Tobbercurry, containing 3,699 inhabitants. It comprises 7,290 statute acres, as applotted under the tithe act, and valued at £2,035 per annum. There is a considerable quantity of mountain

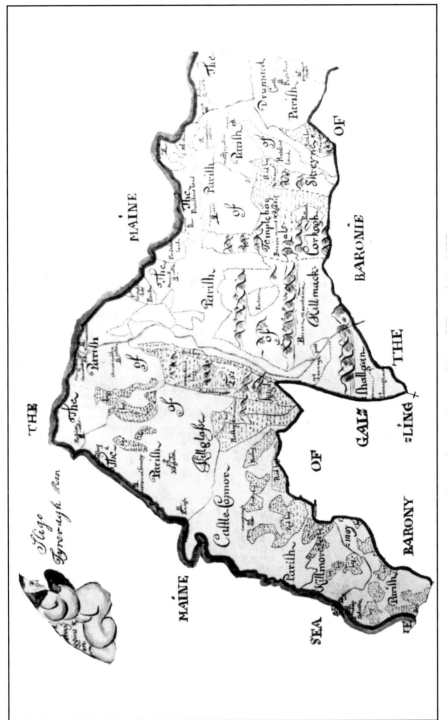

Down Survey; Barony Map of Tireragh (c. 1655)

land and some bog, also limestone. The living is a vicarage, in the diocese of Achonry, united by act of council, in 1819, to that of Kilvarnet, and is in the patronage of the Bishop; the rectory is appropriate to the deanery of Achonry. The tithes amount to £337, of which £131. 10. is payable to the dean, and £215. 10. to the vicar; and the tithes of the benefice amount to £260. 10. The church, which is a small building with a square tower, was erected by aid of a gift of £500 from the late Board of First Fruits in 1766, and has been recently repaired by a grant of £176 from the Ecclesiastical Commissioners. The glebe-house was built by aid of a gift of £200 and a loan of £375 from the late Board, in 1811: the glebe of the union comprises 43a. 3r. 11p. The R. C. parish is co-extensive with that of the Established Church, and has a chapel at Carrownacleigha. There is a meeting-house for Baptists at Coolaney. About 320 children are educated in four public schools, to one of which Major O'Hara contributes £16 and to each of the others £2 annually; and about 110 are educated in two private schools: there are also two Sunday schools.
See COOLANEY

KILMACALLAN, a parish in the barony of Tirerill, 5 miles (S.E.) from Collooney, on the road from that place to Ballyfarnon; containing 4,262 inhabitants. It comprises 6,711 statute acres, of which 5,828 are applotted under the tithe act; the land, which is wet and spongy, is chiefly in tillage, and there is a considerable quantity of bog and marsh. Fairs are held at Castlebaldwin on June 4th and Nov. 3rd. The principal seats are Coopershill, the residence of A.B. Cooper, Esq.; Lakeview, of Wm. Weir, Esq.; and Heapstown, of M. Dillon Manning Esq. It is a prebend, rectory, and vicarage, in the diocese of Elphin: the prebend consists of portions of the tithes of Tawnagh, Drumcolumb, Ballinakill, and Ballysumaghan, amounting to £158. 15. 4; the rectory is impropriate in Viscount Lorton, and the tithes amount to £166. 3. 1., which is equally divided between the impropriator and the vicar; the vicarage forms part of the union of Boyle. The church is a plain building in Riverstown, for the repair of which the Ecclesiastical Commissioners recently granted £183; the Board of First Fruits having given £900 and lent £500 for its erection in 1817. There is a glebe-house, with a glebe 19 acres. In the R. C.

divisions it is the head of a union or district, called Riverstown, comprising this parish, Drumcolumb and Tawnagh, and containing chapels at Riverstown and Ballyrush. There is also a meeting-house for Wesleyan Methodists at Riverstown. About 270 children are educated in three public, and 330 in five private schools; there is also a Sunday school. Part of the old church remains, and the burial-ground is still used as a cemetery.

KILMACOWEN, a parish in the barony of Carbury, 4 miles (S.W.) from Sligo, on the Ballysadare channel; containing 2,296 inhabitants. The name signifies the 'Church of the Sons of Owen'. St. Diarmuid, eldest brother of St. Cormac, founded a church here on lands given by Flann-Dubh, dynast of the Hy-Fiachra. The parish comprises 3.393 statute acres, as applotted under the tithe act, and valued at £5,132 per annum. The soil is light and stony, and the land is principally under tillage: there is a small quantity of bog. Here is Cloverhill, the seat of W. Creighton Chambers, Esq. It is a rectory and vicarage, in the diocese of Elphin, forming part of the union of St. John's Sligo: the tithes amount to £180. 15. 4. In the R.C. divisions it is part of the union or district of St. John's, Sligo. There are two public schools, one of which is supported by Mrs. Chambers. The burial-ground of the old church, which is in ruins, is still used for interment. Here are some druidical altars and cromlechs: and a golden torques found here some time since.

KILMACSHALGAN, a parish in the barony of Tireragh, 16 miles (W. by S.) from Sligo; contains, with the post-town of Dromore West, 3,330 inhabitants. It comprises 25,884 statute acres, the greater portion of which is reclaimable mountain land and bog: the cultivated part is chiefly under tillage. There are quarries of limestone, freestone, and slate. The principal seats are Dromore House, the residence of Capt. J. Fenton; Farranmacfarrell of W. Ormsby, Esq.; Belville, of W. Rutledge, Esq; and Marino Cottage, of T. Ormsby, Esq; Petty sessions are held fortnightly on Thursdays at Camcuil, where there is a spa. The living is a vicarage in the diocese of Killala, with that of Templeboy episcopally united, and in the patronage of Bishop; the rectory is impropriate in Col. Knox Gore. The tithes amount to £499, payable in equal parts to the impropriator and the vicar; and the tithes of the union, to £410. There is a glebe-house, towards the erection of which the late Board of First Fruits gave £100 in 1812; the glebe comprises nine acres. The church is a neat edifice with a square tower, for the erection of which the late Board lent £1,300, in 1820. The R. C. parish co-extensive with that of the Established Church, and has a large unfinished chapel. About 130 children are educated in a public and 140 in three private schools. There are some remains of the old church, with a burial-place attached; two cromlechs and some forts. – See DROMORE WEST.

KILMACTEIGUE, a parish in the barony of Lyney, 6 miles (N. E.) from Foxford, on the road to Ballymote; containing 7,654 inhabitants. It comprises 10,550 statute acres, as applotted under the tithe act. About half the parish is arable and pasture; the remainder is mountain land, with some bog; agriculture is improving. There are some quarries of limestone, which is principally procured for building and repairing the roads. Iron ore from the mountains was smelted at Foxford until the wood used for fuel was exhausted. Fine salmon are taken in the river Moy.; Lough Talt is situated in the midst of high mountains, on which large flocks of goats, &c. feed in summer; it is about a mile long, well stocked with small trout, and contains two small rocky islands, which in summer are covered with gulls. The principal seats are Gleneask, the residence of J. Taaffe, Esq.; and Cloonbarry, of S. Robinson, Esq. The living is a rectory and vicarage, in the diocese of Achonry, and in the gift of the Bishop: the tithes amount to £223. 1. 6. There is a glebe-house, built at an expense of £1300, of which the late Board of First Fruits gave £300 and lent £500, in 1814: the glebe comprises 40 acres. The church is a plain building. The R. C. parish is co-extensive with that of the Established Church, and has chapels at Kilmacteigue and Tourlestrane. There are three public schools, to one of which Mr. Jones has given an acre of land, and in which about 300 children are educated; also a private school, in which are about 70 children, and a Sunday school. At Belclare is an ancient castle. - See BANADA and ACLARE

KILMACTRANNY, a parish in the barony of Tirerill, 6 miles (N.) from Boyle, on the road to Ballyfarnon; containing 4,008 inhabitants. This parish comprises

Sculptured Stone from Ardnaglass
Supposed to be a representation of a Dog killing a Wolf.

Church Island, (Lough Gill) founded by St. Loman in the 6th century,
was partially burned in 1416, when valuable manuscripts, belonging to
the O'Cuirnin scribes, were destroyed.

6,531 statue acres, as applotted under the tithe act, besides which there is much bog and mountain land: the soil is light, and agriculture is in a backward state. Limestone is abundant, iron ore exists, and a seam of coal, 22 inches thick, has lately been discovered in the mountains of Geevagh. It is situated on Lough Arrow, a picturesque sheet of water at the base of the Curlew Mountains, about a mile from Lough Key, by which it communicates with the Shannon: this lake is five miles in length and two in its greatest breadth, and is studded with islands, and remarkable for the size and fine flavour of its trout. On the western side is Hollybrook House, the handsome residence of J. Folliott, Esq., the plantations of which form a pleasing picture when viewed from the opposite shore. Petty sessions are held here every fortnight on Tuesday, and it is a constabulary police station. Kingsborough, which gives the title of Viscount to the eldest son of the Earl of Kingston, is the residence of J. Gethin, Esq.; and Ballinashee, of M. Keogh, Esq. The living is a vicarage of Shancoe, or Shancough, and Killadoon, and in the gift of the bishop; the rectory is impropriate in W. Mulloy, Esq. The tithes amount to £106. 3., which is equally divided between the impropriator and the vicar, and the tithes of the benefice to £89. 11.6. There is a glebe-house, for the erection of which the late Board of First Fruits, in 1819, gave £650 and lent £150: the glebe comprises 12 acres, subject to a rent of £7 per annum. The church is a small modern building, for the erection of which the late Board gave £800, in 1811; and the Ecclesiastical Commissioners have lately granted £305 for its repair.

In the R.C. divisions it is the head of a union or district, called Geevagh, which is co-extensive with the Protestant union, and has a handsome chapel, ornamented with minarets, at Geevagh, and another at Highwood. There are three public schools, to one of which Lord Dundas gave a school-house and garden, and contributes annually, and another is under the patronage of M. Keogh, Esq.; in these schools about 70 children are educated, and there are three private schools, in which are about 170 children. Here is a remarkable cromlech, called 'The Labby' or Diarmuid and Grania's Bed, consisting of a horizontal stone, supported by four others set upright. Among the ruins of the old church is a mutilated cross.

KILMORGAN, a parish in the barony of Corran, 2 miles (E. by N.) from Ballymote, on the road to Dromahaire; contains 2,229 inhabitants. It comprises 5,736 statue acres, principally under tillage, with some pasture land and bog: the soil is generally good, and there is excellent limestone. A manorial court is held on the first Monday in every month. The principal seats are Kilmorgan, the residence of R. Weir, Esq.; Newpark, of R. King Duke Esq., Kilcreevan, of J. Duke, Esq.; and Branchfield, of the Rev. W. Duke. It is a vicarage, in the diocese of Achonry, forming part of the union of Emlaghfad, the rectory is impropriate in Sir H Montgomery, Bart. The tithes amount to £223. 15., of which £103.15. is payable to the impropriator, and £120 to the vicar. In the R. C. divisions it is part of the union or district of Ballymote, and has a chapel at Kilcreevan, and a nunnery. There are two public schools, one of which is aided by an annual donation from H. Clifford, Esq.; about 200 children are educated in them. Part of the old church remains, in which is a large tomb of the McDonagh family, by one of which the church was probably built. Here are several mounds of earth covering stone graves, in which bones and urns containing ashes have been found, whence it is inferred that a battle was anciently fought here.

KILROSS, a parish in the barony of Tirerill, 2 miles (E) from Collooney, on the road to Dromahaire; containing 1,669 inhabitants. The church of the Holy Trinity was built here for Premonstratensian Canons, brough from Lough Key by Clarus Mac Mailin O'Mulconcry, archdeacon of Elphin, in the 13th century: the outer walls still remain, with a burial-place attached. The parish comprises 1,426 statute acres, as applotted under the tithe act, and contains abundance of limestone. Castledargan is the seat of J. Ormsby, Esq., and near it are the ruins of an ancient castle. It is a vicarage in the diocese of Elphin, forming part of the union of Boyle; the rectory is impropriate in Viscount Lorton. The tithes amount to £82. 10. 9 of which £41 is payable to the impropriator, and £41. 10. 9. to the vicar. In the R.C. divisions it forms part of the union or district of Sooey. There are two public schools, in which 140 children are educated, and a private school of about 40.

KILSHALVEY, a parish in the barony of Corran, 8 miles (W.N.W.) from Boyle, on the road to Ballina, containing 2.034 inhabitants. It comprises 5,118 statue acres, as applotted under the tithe act, and principally under tillage: the land is generally good; there is but little bog; limestone is abundant. Atyville is the seat of E. Knott, Esq. It is a vicarage, in the diocese of Achonry, forming part of the union of Killaraght; the rectory is impropriate in the earl of Kingston. The tithes amount to £338. 9. .3, which is equally divided between the impropriator and the vicar. In the R.C, divisions it is part of the union or district of Bunninadden, and has a chapel at Killavill. About 300 children are educated in a national school; and there is another public school at Riverside. There are some remains of the old church.

KILTURRA, a parish, partly in the barony of Costello, county of Mayo, but chiefly in that of Corran, county of Sligo, 5 miles (S. by W.) from Ballymote, on the road to Castlebar; containing 2,481 inhabitants. This parish comprises 7,009 statue acres, as applotted under the tithe act: the land is principally under a gradually improving system of tillage; a large quantity of waste land has been brought into cultivation; there is a considerable extent of bog. Doocastle, the seat of J. M McDonnell Esq., occupies the site of an ancient fortress, of which there are still some remains near the present house. The living is a vicarage, in the diocese of Achonry, forming part of the union of Emlaghfad: the rectory is impropiate in Sir H.C. Montgomery, Bart. The tithes amount to £229. 13.4., of which £109. 7. 6. is payable to the lessee of the impropriator, and £120. 5. 10 to the vicar. In the R. C.divisions the parish forms part of the union or district of Bunninadden. There are two private schools, in which are about 200 children. There are numerous Danish raths in the parish; and about three miles westward from Collooney are the remains of Meemlough castle, built by T.B O'Hara; the walls are still entire and are perforated by flights of steps.

KILVARNET, a parish in the barony of Leyny, 5 miles (N. by W.) from Ballymote, on the mountain road from Sligo to Ballina, containing 2,360 inhabitants. This parish, which is situated on the river Owenmore, comprises 2.465 statue acres. As

The 'Lady of the Lake', which plied between Sligo and Dromahaire in the mid 19th century, seen here berthed at the Riverside, Sligo.

applotted under the tithe act. The surface is mountainous, and agriculture is in a backward state, but a considerable tract of mountain is gradually being reclaimed; there is a moderate quantity of bog, but little more than what is requisite for fuel; limestone is quarried both for building and agricultural purposes. The principal seats are Templehouse, that of Col. A. Perceval, a handsome modern mansion, on the border of a fine lake and in an extensive and well-planted demesne, in which the ruins of the ancient house of Knights Templars, from which it takes its name, form an interesting object on the margin of the lake; Annaghmore, of Major C. K. O'Hara, a handsome residence delightfully situated in an ample demesne enlivened by the windings of the river Owenmore, over which is a handsome bridge, and commanding a fine view of the course of the river, the distant hills of Knocknarea and Benbulben, the Ox mountains, and the picturesque hills of Knocknashee and Muckelty, with much of the fine country in the neighbourhood; and Somerton of the Rev. T.D. Carroll. The linen manufacture is carried on by individuals to a small extent, and there is a bleach-green at Ballinacarrow, where fairs are held on May 19th, June 16th, Oct. 14th, and Dec. 14th for cattle, pigs, and yarn; fairs are also held at Templehouse. Petty sessions are held at Coolaney, where a penny post has been established. It is a vicarage, in the diocese of Achonry, forming part of the union of Killoran; the rectory is appropriate to the deanery. The tithes amount to £76.12.3., of which £35. 1. 6. is payable to the Dean of Achonry, and the remainder to the vicar. In the R. C. divisions it is part of the union or district of Collooney; the chapel is at Ballinacarrow. There is a place of worship for Baptists. About 400 children are taught in four public schools, of which two are supported by Col. Perceval and Major O'Hara; and there is a private school, in which are about 50 children. The preceptory of Knights Templars, anciently called Drumabradh and subsequently *Teachtemple*, was founded in the reign of Henry 111., and on the suppression of that order was given by Edw. 11 to the Knights Hospitallers. There are also some ruins of the old churches of Killoran and Kilvarnet.

MULLAGHMORE,

a peninsulated district, in the parish of Ahamlish, 9 miles (N.) from Sligo: the population is returned with the parish. This place, which is situated on the north-western coast, near Milkhaven, and includes several small villages, has been greatly improved by Viscount Palmerston, who has built here a commodious quay, from which the inhabitants export corn and other agricultural produce; and has also expended considerably sums in reclaiming the neighbouring bogs, and in planting the loose sands with that species of grass called 'bent,' which alone will take root, and render them in due time a firm and solid beach. His lordship has built several neat houses for the reception of families during the bathing season and a new town is rapidly springing up near the quay, which will soon supersede the villages of Ballintemple and Grange.

OYSTER-ISLAND,

in the parish of Killaspugbrone, 5 miles (N. N. W.) from Sligo: the population is returned with the parish. It is situated in the 'Pool of Sligo.' And is remarkable for the purity of its herbage, and for restoring diseased cattle. Its ancient name was Inishroras, and it is enumerated among the lands granted by Chas. 11 to the Earl of Strafford and Thomas Radcliffe Esq., in 1666.

RAUGHLEY,

a village, in the parish of Drumcliffe, 10 miles (N.W.) from Sligo; containing 122 inhabitants. This place, which is situated on the north side of the bay of Sligo, takes its name from a small elevated peninsula connected with the sand hills on the shore by a long narrow isthmus; and having on the south-west side the Wheaten Rock, which extends nearly half a mile to the north-east and south-west, and is partly dry at spring tides; and off the south end, the Bird Rocks, about two cables' length from the shore. A pier has been erected by the government, which affords great accommodation to vessels trading with Sligo, and to the boats engaged in the fisheries off this coast, in which more than 200 persons are occasionally employed; large quantities of sea manure are landed at the pier, which is within half a mile of the nearest public road, and a coast-guard station is placed here, forming one of the five that constitute the district of Sligo. The village contains 25 dwellings, most of which are thatched cabins. Near it is Rockly Lodge, the residence of

John Jones Esq. Near the western shore is the romantic hill of Knocklane, under which are some remains of fortifications; and on the eastern shore, about half a mile from the village, are the ruins of the old castle of Ardtarmon, now deeply buried in the sand, the ancient residence of the Gore family. The blowing sands of Knocklane extend northward from the village, and are about two miles long and two broad; they have already covered a great tract of good land and about 150 cabins, and are constantly in motion, giving a dreary and desolate appearance to the country around. On the western shore is a remarkable chasm in the limestone rock, called the Pigeon Holes, into which the seal rushes with great impetuosity, and in rough weather is forced upwards to a considerable height. Close to the shore is a chalybeate spring of great strength, which is sometimes covered by the tide.

RIVERSTOWN, a village, partly in the parish of Drumcolumb, but chiefly in that of Kilmacallan, on the road from Collooney to Ballyfarnon; containing 89 houses and 421 inhabitants. It is a constabulary police station, and contains the parish church, (a plain building), a meeting house for Methodists, and a dispensary. It is the head of a R.C. union or district, comprising this parish and those of Tawnagh and Drumcolumb, in which union are two chapels; that in Riverstown is a plain building.

ROSSES (UPPER and LOWER), two villages in the parish of Drumcliffe, 5 miles (N.N.W.) from Sligo, the former containing 170 inhabitants: the population of the latter is returned with the parish. They are situated on the peninsula that separates the 'Pool of Sligo' from the bay of Drumcliffe On the shore of the former are several bathing-lodges for the accommodation of visitors during the season; and in the vicinity is the race course of Bomore where races are held by subscription, generally in August.

ST. JOHN'S, a parish in the barony of Carbury, containing, with the greater part of the Borough and sea-port town of Sligo, 12,982 inhabitants, of which number, 11,411, are in the Town. The parish comprises 4,350 statute acres, as applotted under the tithe act, and valued at £7,056 per annum. The rural part consists generally of good land, contains excellent limestone, and is

Tobernalt Holy Well - a relic of Penal Times

embellished with many handsome houses and demesnes, which command fine views of the bay of Sligo, with the two magnificent headlands, Benbulben and Knocknarea, that form its entrance; the latter of these is said to derive its name, which signifies 'The King's Hill,' from having been the place where the kings of Ireland were anciently inaugurated. The principal seats are noticed in the article on the Town of Sligo, which see. The living is a rectory and vicarage, in the diocese of Elphin, united in 1681 to the vicarage of Calry and the rectories and vicarages of Killaspugbrone and Kilmacowen, and in the patronage of the Bishop: the tithes amount to £341. 10. 9. and of the entire benefice to £870. 11. 8. There is a glebe-house, with an acre of glebe. The church was built in 1730 on the site of an earlier edifice erected by Sir Roger Jones, from a design by the German architect, Cassels. In 1812 it was remodelled, at a cost of £5,059, and transformed into a Gothic structure. In the R. C. divisions the parish is the head of a union or district, called Sligo and Calry, comprising the parishes of St. John, Calry, Killaspugbrone and Kilmacowen, and containing chapels at Sligo, Calry, and Ransboro, and a small Dominician convent with a chapel in Sligo.

There is a meeting-house for Presbyterians in connection with the Synod of Ulster, of the third class, also meeting-houses for Independents and Primitive Methodists. About 780 children are educated in five public schools, and in two which are in the county gaol and about 580 in fifteen private schools; there are also six Sunday schools

SHANCOE, or SHANCOUGH, a parish, in the barony of Tirerill, 9 miles (N. by E.) from Boyle, on the road from Sligo to Ballyfarnon; containing 1,208 inhabitants. It is on the confines of the county of Leitrim, and comprises 8,900 statute acres, as applotted under the tithe act, of which a large portion consists of mountain and bog; some of the land, however, is good; limestone abounds, and iron-ore is supposed to exist in the mountains. It is a vicarage, in the diocese of Elphin, forming part of the union of Kilmactranny; the rectory is impropriate to Alex. Perceval, Esq. The tithes, amounting to £33. 4. 7., are payable in equal portions to the impropriator and vicar. In the R. C. divisions the parish forms part of the union or district of Kilmactranny. A 'Patron' is annually held on July 25th at St. James's Well.

SKREEN, a parish in the barony of Tireragh, 5 miles (E) from Dromore West, on the road from Sligo to Ballina, and on Ardnaglass harbour; containing 4,567 inhabitants. This parish was anciently called *Knock-na-moile*, and was granted by Tipriak, Chief of Hy-Fiachra, to St. Columb: it obtained its present name from a shrine of St. Adamnan erected here. From its contiguity to the shore of the Atlantic, great facility is afforded of obtaining valuable manure: agriculture is very bad, the peasantry being adverse to the adoption of any improvements, though the land is in itself good; there is some bog in the mountains. At Ardnaglass is a good limestone quarry, from which some of the hewn stone work of the new chapel at Ballina was procured; it bears the chisel well and takes a good polish. Petty sessions are held at Ardnaglass once a fortnight; and fairs for cattle on June 21st, Aug. 13th, Sept. 23rd, and Nov. 12th. Leekfield is residence of Lewis G. Jones, Esq.; Seafort of R. Wood, Esq.; and Tubberpatrick of Jeremiah Jones, Esq. The living is a rectory and vicarage, in the diocese of Killala, and in the patronage of the Archbishop of Tuam; the tithes amount to £480. The glebe-house was built in 1807 by the then incumbent, at a cost of £680; the glebe comprises 21 acres, valued at £52. 10. per annum. The church is a neat excellent preservation building with a square tower, and was erected in 1819, near the ruins of the former, by aid of a loan of £1,200 from the late Board of First Fruits: the Ecclesiastical Commissioners have lately granted £180 for its repair. The R. C. parish is co-extensive with that of the Established Church, and contains a chapel. On the glebe is a female school aided by the incumbent; a school at Farniharpy is under the patronage of the Rev. T. Webber, who built the school-house; and there are four other public schools, in all which about 280 children are taught. There are also three private schools, in which are about 210 children. Tradition reports that once there were seven churches within the parish, and that there existed an establishment for religious instruction; there are appearances of the foundations of many buildings. The old castle of Ardnaglass, of which there are considerable remains, was originally the residence of the O'Dowds, a family then of great note, and was also in the possession of the McSweeneys; it is now the property of J. Jones,

The Skreen Monument stands on the roadside close to the churchyard. It bears a Latin inscription which translated literally reads "Eugene McDonnell, Vicar of this district, had me erected, 1591.

Esq., whose ancestor came over with Oliver Cromwell. At Skreen is a very fine well, having over it a monument inscribed, *"Eugenius Mc Donnail vacarius hujus vile, M.F.F. 1591:"* it is in excellent preservation.

TAWNAGH, a parish in the barony of Tirerill, 9 miles (N.N.W.) from Boyle, on the road to Sligo; containing 1,568 inhabitants. This parish, situated on the river Arrow, or Unshin, which flows from Lough Arrow, comprises, as applotted under the tithe act, 2,510 statute acres; it has in general a good deep soil, and contains a small quantity of bog. It is in the diocese of Elphin; the rectory forms part of the union and corps of the prebend of Kilmacallan, the vicarage, part of the union of Boyle. The tithes amount to £77. 10. 9., equally divided between the rector and the vicar. In the R. C. divisions it is part of the union or district called Riverstown. There are remains of the old church, with a burial-ground attached; and near the mail coach road are the ruins of Behy castle, surrounded with trees. A patron is held at Patrick's Well on March 17th.

TEMPLEBOY, a parish in the barony of Tireragh, 3 miles (E) from Dromore-West, on the mail coach road to Ballina; containing 3,787 inhabitants. This parish, which is situated at the entrance of the bay of Sligo, and includes within its limits the point or headland of Aughris, comprises 13,388 statute acres, as applotted under the tithe act. A large portion is mountainous, and there is a considerable tract of bog; the land is generally of good quality and principally under tillage, but the system of agriculture is not improved. There are quarries of stone of good quality for building, and also of slate. The principal seats are Seaview House, the residence of W. H. Hillas, Esq.; Corkhill of Capt. Moore; Grange, of J. Black, Esq.: and Donaghintraine, of V. Jones, Esq. The entrance of the bay of Sligo, from the headland of Aughris to the point of Rinoran, is about five miles wide; and the shores of the parish, which are bold and rocky, are curiously indented with natural caverns excavated by the action of the waves. One of these, called Seals' Hole, from the number of seals which frequent it, is nearly half a mile in length, rising in some parts more than 15 feet above the water, which rushes into it with great violence. The cavern called Coragh Dtonn, or 'the iron chest,' extends to a considerable distance under the cliff, and is frequently visited by strangers; a small landing-place has been made near it by the coast-guard, enabling small fishing boats from the Donegal coast to land in safety. At Pullendiva is a coast-guard station, one of the five that constitute the district of Sligo. A manorial court is held at Seaview House, it is a vicarage, in the diocese of Killala, forming part of the union of Kilmacshalgan; the rectory is impropriate to R. W. Hillas, Esq., of Dublin. The tithes amount to £560, of which £350, is payable to the impropriator, and the remainder to the vicar. The R. C. parish is co-extensive with that of the Established Church. There are five private schools, in which are about 300 children. A priory of Augustine canons was founded in 1280, at Aughris, by the family of Mac Donald, the prior of which was, in 1544, consecrated Bishop of Elphin. In a field near Grange a gold signet ring, weighing nearly an ounce, was dug up by a labourer, some years since, and is now in the possession of Mr. Thomas Hillas, late of Seaview House.

TOOMOUR, a parish, in the barony of Corran, 5 miles (N.W.) from Boyle, on the road to Ballymote; containing 3,395 inhabitants. It comprises 8,496 statute acres, as applotted under the tithe act. The portion of the land which is under cultivation, both in tillage and pasture, is of superior quality and makes a good return, but there is a good deal of mountain and bog: limestone is abundant for all purposes. Battlefield is the residence of James Knott, Esq.; and Mount Dodwell, of C. Thompson, Esq. It is a vicarage, in the diocese of Achonry, forming part of the union of Emlaghfad; the rectory is impropriate in Sir H. C. Montgomery, Bart. The tithes amount to £294. 5. of which £124. 5. is payable to the impropriator, and £170 to the vicar. In the R.C. divisions it is the head of a union or district, called Keash, which comprises this parish and that of Drumrat: the chapel at Keash, in Toomour parish, is a large building in good repair. There is a place of worship belonging to a Presbyterian congregation at Graniamore; where also there is a school, and there is a national school at Templevaney: about 140 boys and 79 girls are educated in these schools. The remains of an old church with a burial-ground are at Toomour, and another ruin and

St. Crumnathy's Cathedral, Achonry, a plain edifice with a tower and a spire, built in 1823, and reputedly the smallest Cathedral in Europe.

enclosure of similar character is at Templevaney. The lofty hill of Keash contains several remarkable caves, some of which extend to a considerable length: the entrance to the largest is 30 feet high.

TUBBERCURRY, a chapelry, in the parish of Achonry, about 8 miles (S.W.) from Ballymote, on the road from Boyle to Ballina; containing 650 inhabitants. The village, which comprises 90 houses, of which only 15 are slated, has a penny post to Ballymote, and a dispensary; it is a constabulary police station, and petty sessions are held in it every Thursday. There is a market on Monday; and fairs are held on Feb.

6th, March 25th, May 22nd, June 27th, Aug. 15th, Oct 4th and Nov. 29th. The chapel is a neat building with an octagonal tower, erected in 1830 by aid of a gift of £900 from the late Board of First Fruits: it is built of limestone (procured in a quarry in the parish) in the Gothic style, and stands on a commanding eminence. The curate is appointed by the Dean of Achonry, and has a stipend of £75 per annum.

TUBBERSCANAVAN, a village in the parish of Ballysadare, 1 mile (S.E.) from Collooney, on the road from Boyle to Sligo; containing 48 houses and 233 inhabitants. Fairs are held on May 17th, June 30th, Sept. 19th, and Oct. 31st.

A pre-historic monument at Carrowmore